The British Museum
Occasional Paper
Number 98

Catalogue of Punic Stelae in The British Museum

Carole Mendleson

The British Museum
Occasional Papers

Publishers
The British Museum
Great Russell Street
London WC1B 3DG

Production Editor
Dr Josephine Turquet

Assistant Editor
Yasuyo Ohta

Occasional Paper No. 98,
Catalogue of Punic Stelae in The British Museum

Carole Mendleson

ISBN 0 86159 098 8
ISSNISSN 0142 4815

Front cover: The tophet at Carthage as it is today.
(Photo: Jonathan N. Tubb)

For a complete catalogue giving information on the full range
of available Occasional Papers please see the Occasional Papers
website: www/the britishmuseum.ac.uk/occasionalpapers
or write to:
Oxbow Books
Park End Place
Oxford OX1 1HN
UK
Tel: (+44) (0) 1865 241249
Fax (+44) (0) 1865 794449
e mail oxbow@oxbowbooks.com
website www.oxbowbooks.com
or
The David Brown Book Co
PO Box 511
Oakville
CT 06779
USA
Tel: (+1) 860 945 9329; Toll free 1 800 791 9354
Fax: (+1) 860 945 9468
e mail david.brown.bk.co@snet.net

Printed and bound in the UK by The Chameleon Press Limited

Preface v
John Curtis, Keeper, Department of the Ancient Near East, the British Museum

Foreword and Acknowledgements v
Carole Mendleson

List of Abbreviations vi

Introduction 1
- **Punic civilization** 1
- **Origins of the collection** 1
- **Technique** 3
- **Material** 3
- **Stela function** 4
- **Punic and neo-Punic** 4
- **Inscriptions** 4
- **Provenance of the neo-Punic stelae** 4

Iconography 7
- **Punic period (4th–2nd centuries BC)** 7
- **The neo-Punic period (2nd century BC–3rd century AD)** 10
- **Index of iconographic symbols** 13
  - **Symbols on Punic stelae**
  - **Symbols on neo-Punic stelae**

Catalogue 19
- **Tomb markers** 19
- **Punic stelae** 21
- **Neo-Punic stelae** 37

Personal Names 49

Concordances of Numbers 53
- **1. Museum numbers and catalogue numbers** 53
- **2. Departmental and registration numbers and list of inscriptions** 55

Appendix 1
The 'Honegger' Collection 59

Appendix 2
Extract of Letter from Nathan Davis to Lord Clarendon 61

Appendix 3
Copy of Letter from Sir Grenville Temple in *Transactions of the Royal Asiatic Society* 1835 62

Appendix 4
Report on the Examination of Punic and Neo-Punic Stelae from Carthage 63
Andrew Middleton, Department of Scientific Research, The British Museum

Plates 65
Tomb markers 65
Punic stelae 67
Neo-Punic stelae 97

Preface

Included in this volume are nearly 200 limestone stelae in the British Museum from Carthage in Tunisia and surrounding areas of North Africa. Many of the stelae were acquired by the Reverend Nathan Davis who excavated at about 20 different sites in and around Carthage between 1856 and 1858. Others come from the interior of Tunisia and from Algeria. The majority of the stelae have votive or dedicatory inscriptions in Punic and some of them are thought to come from tophets, burial precincts that are characteristic of Phoenician settlements in the West Mediterranean. The stelae date from between about the 4th century BC and the 4th century AD and in the catalogue they are divided into Punic and Neo-Punic, according to whether they pre- or post-date the Roman sack of Carthage in 146 BC.

This catalogue is the work of Carole Mendleson who was a curator in the Department of Western Asiatic Antiquities (now the Department of the Ancient Near East) at the British Museum from 1967 until 1997. She is already well-known in Phoenician studies as the joint editor (with R.D. Barnett) of *Tharros: A Catalogue of Material in the British Museum from Phoenician and Other Tombs at Tharros, Sardinia* (British Museum Publications 1987). Most of the photographs in this publication were taken by Barbara Winter and the modern line-drawings are by Ann Searight. The volume has been helped through the press by Jonathan Tubb, but above all thanks are due to Josephine Turquet, the production editor of the British Museum Occasional Papers, who has handled the project with her usual flair and efficiency.

John Curtis,
Keeper, Department of the Ancient Near East

Foreword and Acknowledgements

Most of the stelae and monuments in this volume have been previously published, especially those with inscriptions, but these publications have generally been to discuss either the inscription or the iconography but not both and the possible connections between the two have not been seriously examined until fairly recently.

We have tried to provide as much new information as possible, mainly through the discovery of the original correspondence relating to the acquisition and provenance of the stelae, especially those of the neo-Punic period which were acquired by purchase in the mid-19th century, the provenance of which has long been subject to discussion. All the stelae have been restudied by the author. In a very few cases the stone appears to have deteriorated so that the original readings cannot be checked but on the whole they are in good condition.

The transcriptions and translations of the Punic and neo-Punic inscriptions have for the most part been those used in BMPI, *CIS* and in Chabot *Punica* except where there has been an obvious error noted during the physical examination of the stela. I am very grateful for the assistance of the late Dr Michael Weizman who checked the transcriptions and transliterations of the inscriptions on the Punic stelae. Professor Maurice Sznycer of the École Pratique des Hautes Études, Paris and Professor Maria Giulia Amadasi Guzzo of the University of Rome between them undertook the task of restudying the neo-Punic inscriptions and we are grateful for their contributions. My thanks also to Professor Paul Mosca of the University of British Colombia and Professor Felice Israel of the University of Genoa for their most helpful advice.

If there are any glaring epigraphic errors it is entirely due to the author. Bearing in mind that not everyone who reads this volume will be familiar with the diacritics used in Semitic epigraphy we have tried to use the most common forms of vocalization deriving from transcriptions in Greek and Latin in the translation of the names. We realize that the correct pronounciation of names is still a matter of some debate but what we have tried to do is make it easier for the lay reader to understand by, in most cases, using the most familiar forms.

Carole Mendleson

List of Abbreviations

AA	Antiquités africaines
Alaoui 1897	F. du Coudray La Blanchère and P. Gauckler, *Catalogue du Musée Alaoui* (Paris 1897)
Alaoui 1954	C. Gilbert Picard, *Catalogue du Musée Alaoui, Nouvelle Série* (Collections Puniques) T.1 (Tunis 1954)
Benz, 1972	F.L. Benz, *Personal Names in ithe Phoenician and Punic Inscriptions* (Rome 1972)
Berthier-Charlier 1952	A. Berthier & R. Charlier, *Le sanctuaire punique d'El Hofra à Constantine* (Paris 1952)
Bertrandy-Sznycer 1987	F. Bertrandy & M. Sznycer, *Les stèles puniques de Constantine* (Paris 1987)
Bisi 1967	A.M. Bisi, *Le stele puniche*, Studi Semitici 27 (Rome 1967)
Bisi 1976	A.M. Bisi, Su un gruppo di stele neo-puniche del British Museum, *Rivista di Studi Fenici* 4, 1 (1976), 23-40
Bisi 1978	A.M. Bisi, A proposito di alcune stele del tipo della Ghorfa al British Museum, *Antiquités africaines* 12 (1978), 21-88
BMPI 1863	W.S.W. Vaux, *Inscriptions in the Phoenician Character now Deposited in the British Museum Discovered on the Site of Carthage During Researches made by Nathan Davis Esq. at the Expense of Her Majesty's Government in the Years 1856, 1857 and 1858* (London 1863)
Bourgade 1852	F. Bourgade, *Toison d'Or de la langue Phénicienne* (Paris 1852)
Brown 1991	S. Brown, *Late Carthaginian Child Sacrifice* (Sheffield 1991)
C.I.L.	*Corpus Inscriptionum Latinarum* (Berlin 1863-)
CIS	*Corpus Inscriptionum Semiticarum, Pars Prima* (Paris 1881-1962)
Chabot 1916a	J.B. Chabot, Punica I-V, *Journal Asiatique* 7 (Jan-Fév 1916), 77-109
Chabot 1916b	J.B. Chabot, Punica VI-X, *Journal Asiatique* 7 (Mai-Juin 1916), 443-67
Chabot 1916c	J.B. Chabot, Punica XI, *Journal Asiatique* 8 (Nov-Déc 1916), 483-520
Chabot 1917a	J.B. Chabot, Punica XII, *Journal Asiatique* 9 (Jan-Fév 1917), 145-66
Chabot 1917b	J.B. Chabot, Punica XIII-XVIII, *Journal Asiatique* 10 (Juillet-Août 1917), 5-79
Chabot, *Punica*	Extracts from the *Journal Asiatique* 1916-1918 (Paris 1918)
Charlier 1953	R. Charlier, Les stèles puniques de Constantine et la question des sacrifice dits 'Molchomor' en relation avec l'expression 'BSHRMBTM', *Karthago* IV (1953), 1-48
Cintas 1970	P. Cintas, *Manuel d'Archéologie Punique* I (Paris 1970)
Cintas 1976	P. Cintas, *Manuel d'Archéologie Punique* II (Paris 1976)
Cooke 1903	G.A. Cooke, *A Text-Book of North Semitic Inscriptions* (Oxford 1903)
Davis 1861	N. Davis, *Carthage and her Remains* (London 1861)
Euting 1871	J. Euting, Punische Steine, *Mémoires de l'Académie des Sciences de St Pétersburg*, VIIIe série, tome XVII, no. 3 (1871)
Euting 1883	J. Euting, *Sammlung der Carthagischen Inschriften* I (Strassburg 1883)
Gesenius 1837	W. Gesenius, *Scripturae Linguaeque Phoeniciae Monumenta quotquot supersunt* (Leipzig 1837)
Goodenough 1954	E.R. Goodenough, Jewish Symbols in the Greco-Roman Period, vol. 4 (New York 1954)
Harden 1962	D. Harden, *The Phoenicians* (London 1962)
Harden 1980	D. Harden, *The Phoenicians,* rev. edn. (1980)
Hoftijzer-Jongeling	J. Hoftijzer and K. Jongeling, *Dictionary of the North-West Semitic Inscriptions* (Leiden 1995)
Hours-Miédan 1951	M. Hours-Miédan, Les représentations figurées sur les stèles de Carthage, *Cahiers de Byrsa* I (1951), 15-160
IRTS 20	J.M. Reynolds, Inscriptions of Roman Tripolitania, A Supplement, *PBSR* 23 [1955]
Jongeling 1984	K. Jongeling, *Names in Neo-Punic Inscriptions.* (Groningen 1984)
Jongeling 1994	K. Jongeling, *North African Names from Latin Sources* (Leiden 1994)
KAI	H. Donner and W Röllig, *Kanaanische und aramäaische Inschriften,* 3 vols (Wiesbaden 1962-64)
Kelsey 1926	W.F. Kelsey, *Excavations at Carthage 1925* (New York 1926)
Kitzinger 1969	*Early Medieval Art* (London 1969)
Leglay 1961	M. Leglay, *Saturne Africain, Monuments*, Tome 1, *Afrique Proconsulaire* (Paris 1961)
Leglay 1966	M. Leglay, *Saturne Africain, Histoire*, Bibliothèque des Écoles Françaises d'Athènes et de Rome, Fasc. 205, (Paris 1966)
Leglay 1984	M. Leglay, Les religions de l'Afrique romaine au IIe siècle d'après Apulée et les inscriptions, in *L'Africa Romana*, Atti del I convegno di Studio (Sassari 1984), 47-61, pls. I-VIII
Lidzbarski 1898	M. Lidzbarski, *Handbuch der Nordsemitischen Epigraphik* (Weimar 1898)
M'charek 1988	A. M'charek, Maghrawa, lieu de provenance des stèles punico-numides dites de la Ghorfa, in *Mélanges de l'École Française de Rome*, 100 (1988) - 2, 731-60
M'charek 1995	A. M'charek, La romanisation du culte de Ba'al Hammon dans la région de Maktar (Antique Thusca), in *Actes du IIIe Congrès International des Études Phéniciennes et Puniques*, vol. II (Tunis 1995)
Mendleson 1995	C. Mendleson, Punic Stelae in the British Museum, in *Actes du IIIe Congrès International des Études Phéniciennes et Puniques*, vol. II (Tunis 1995)
PBSR	*Papers of the British School at Rome*
Phoenicians 1988	*The Phoenicians* (Milan 1988)
Picard 1957	G-C. Picard, Civitas Mactaritana, *Karthago* VIII (1957) 42-47
Picard 1976	C. Picard, Les représentations du sacrifice molk sur les ex-voto de Carthage, *Karthago* XVII (1973- 4), 67-138
Picard 1978	C. Picard, Les représentations du sacrifice molk sur les stèles de Carthage (suite et fin), *Karthago* XVIII (1975-6) [1978], pls. XIII-XXIV, pp. 5-116
RIL	J.B. Chabot, *Recueil des Inscriptions Libyques* (Paris 1940)
Sader 1991	H. Sader, Phoenician Stelae From Tyre, *Berytus* XXXIX (1991), 101-26
Schröder 1869	P. Schröder, *Die Phönizische Sprache* (Halle 1869)
Segert 1976	S. Segert, *A Grammar of Phoenician and Punic* (Munich 1976)
Tomback 1978	R. Tomback, *A Comparative Semitic Lexicon of the Phoenician and Punic Languages* (New York 1978)
Winstanley 1850	Messrs Winstanley and Sons, *A Catalogue of Interesting Antiquities Excavated in the Years 1835 and 1836 from Ruined Temples of Carthage...* (Liverpool 1850)
Wright 1886	W. Wright, Note on Seven Punic Inscriptions in the British Museum, *Proceedings of the Society of Biblical Archaeology*, June 1886, 211-13

Introduction

Punic civilization

Punic is the word generally used as a description of the Phoenician culture of the western Mediterranean. It comes from the Latin name for the Phoenicians, *Poeni*, and is applied to the descendants of the founders of Carthage, who themselves settled all over the western Mediterranean. Sailing from their native city-states of Tyre and Sidon during the 1st millennium BC, and possibly even earlier, the Phoenicians first founded trading-posts and then colonies, establishing a network which eventually extended throughout the Mediterranean – from Cyprus and the Levant coast in the east through the Straits of Gibraltar and to the Atlantic coasts of Iberia and Africa in the west – in a search for the raw materials such as copper, tin, ivory and precious metals from which they made the exquisite objects for which they were renowned. Carthage, founded by settlers from Tyre, was the largest and greatest of Phoenician colonies. Its inhabitants created a far-flung empire that rivalled that of the Greeks and the Romans.

By an odd quirk of history we know more about the Phoenicians from what has been found in their colonies than we do from their homeland. This is partly because the original Phoenician cities of the Lebanon are still inhabited by their descendants, thus making properly controlled excavation difficult, and partly because the recent troubled history of that country has hindered excavation. This is gradually being remedied with modern excavations by a new generation of archaeologists in Lebanon.

The Phoenicians were great maritime traders and explorers and superb craftsmen but perhaps their most enduring contribution to civilisation was the development of the alphabet. However, although they were a literate people, almost all their written works have disappeared and we know of them mainly from Classical sources. The main evidence we have for the Phoenician language comes from their stone monuments and consists mostly of comparatively short inscriptions carved on stelae, many of which were found at Carthage and other sites in North Africa.

One of the most recognisable features of Punic culture which has been found in almost every large Phoenician settlement in the west is a sacred open-air burial precinct known as a tophet. Here have been found the ashes of thousands of infants, children and animals, carefully placed in lidded jars and buried, in the early years covered with a pile of small stones and later with a votive stone (stela) above ground. It is thought by many that these ashes are the remains of sacrifices to the Punic gods Tanit and Baal Hammon. The stela often has an engraved inscription of dedication to one or both of these deities in fulfilment of a vow.

At most sites the tophet came into being shortly after the foundation of a settlement; it continued to be used in North Africa wherever there was Punic settlement long after the defeat and destruction of Carthage by the Romans in 146 BC.

Origins of the collection

The Department of Ancient Near East in the British Museum has in its collections almost 200 Punic and neo-Punic stelae from North Africa, all acquired during the 19th century. The bulk of the collection comes from the excavations of the Rev. Nathan Davis during the 1850s on behalf of the British Government.[1] He excavated at about 20 different sites in and around Carthage and also obtained stelae by purchase.[2] He also acquired inscribed stelae in the interior through a Mr Crow, Vice-Consul of Benghazi and then Susa (Sousse); these are said to come partly from near Zama, Le Kef (Sicca Veneria) and Baja (Vacca) and, in his correspondence with the British Museum,[3] Davis writes that they were excavated by J.B. Honegger.[4] They are almost certainly neo-Punic and the fact that Davis says in his book that the stelae were inscribed may indicate that NPu3-17 were part of this group.

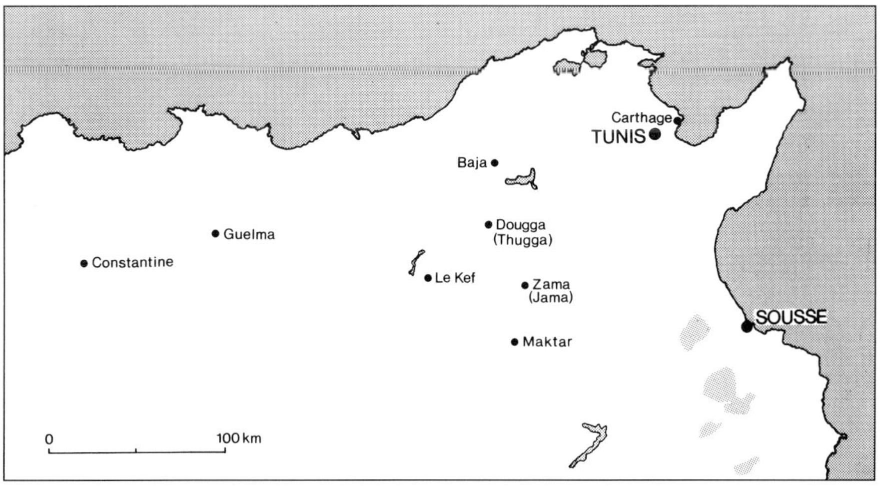

Figure 1 Map of Northern Africa showing relevant sites

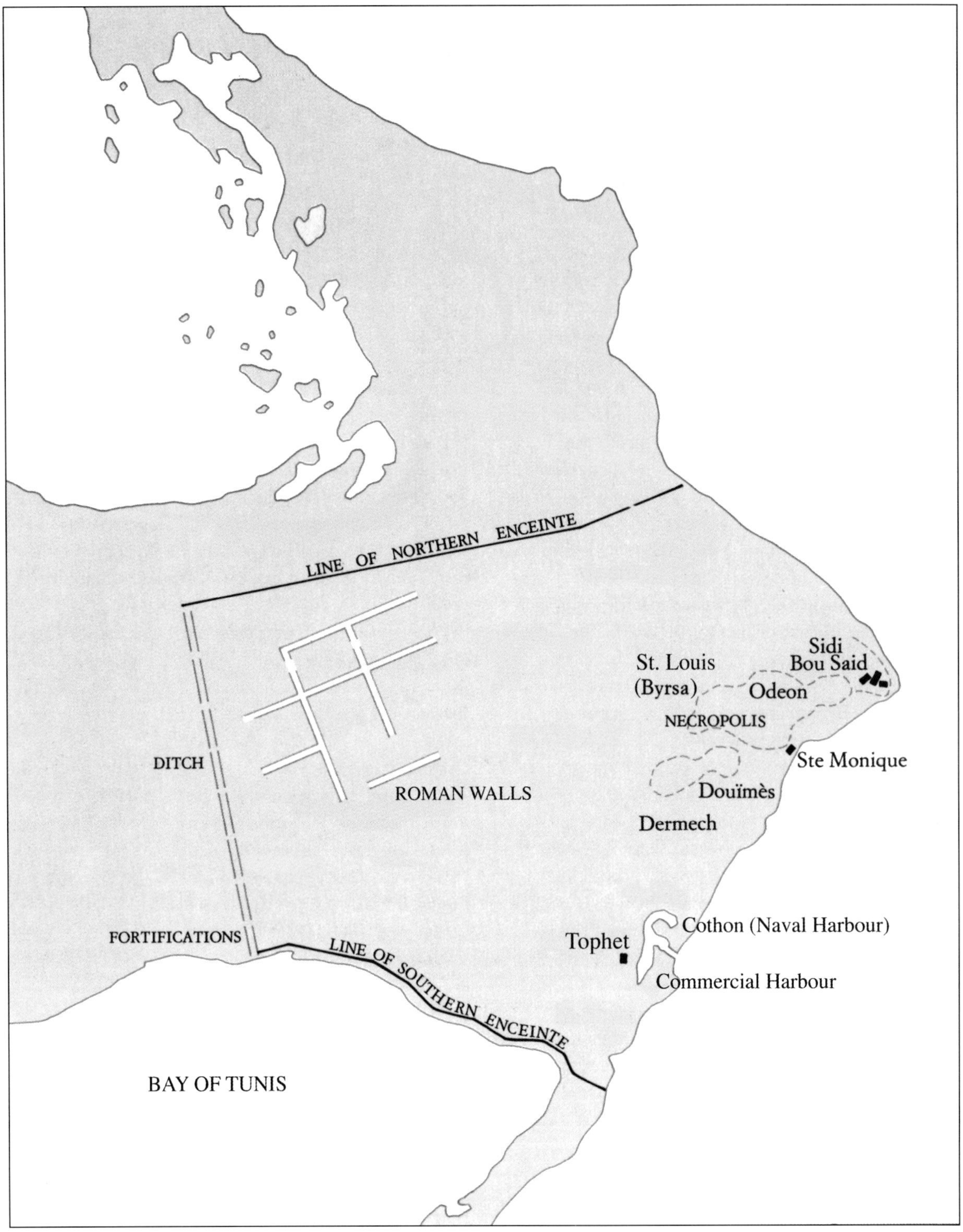

Figure 2 Ancient Carthage

Most of the stelae Davis found at Carthage came from between the hill of St Louis and the sea (see map, **Fig. 2**).[5] In his book[6] he describes how he found over 100 stelae built into a Roman wall.[7] It is now known that these came originally from the upper layers of the tophet, which was discovered in 1921.[8] When the stelae first began to turn up at Carthage, it was not known what they were. Vaux, in the preface to BMPI, recognises them as votive and not funerary. At the time their importance lay in the inscriptions; until then very few Phoenician inscriptions had been found. To quote from the preface,

> With reference to the value of this collection... there were scarcely twenty inscriptions unquestionably Carthaginian in the various museums of Europe and there have been... considerable differences of opinion... owing to the uncertainty existing as to the form of particular letters.

The stelae found by Davis at Carthage are a small proportion of the thousands of stelae from the tophet found re-used in different parts of Carthage over the years, both before and after the tophet was discovered, and those found *in situ* later. Most of the remainder, including many neo-Punic stelae, were also acquired during his stay in North Africa. Unfortunately, apart from those illustrated in his book and published in BMPI we can but guess at their provenance.

Other stelae obtained by Davis came from discoveries by J.B. Honegger, a German architect in the service of the Pasha of Tunis, who also conducted excavations for Sir Thomas Reade, at one time British Consul at Tunis. Nine of the 13 stelae from the Reade collection were acquired in 1850, the others in 1858. Nine stelae, acquired in 1876, came from the Fenner collection, all said to be from Carthage. Another group of 14 Punic stelae said to come from Carthage was acquired in 1886.

Unfortunately the Museum's collection was acquired long before the days of systematic archaeological excavation and proper recording of provenance was not considered very important. This has led to much speculation over the years, especially about the problem of the provenance of the neo-Punic stelae.

We are confident that the Punic stelae published in BMPI are from Carthage. However, in his preface Vaux states (about unpublished stelae):

> ... Some of these late Phoenician inscriptions were purchased at different times by Mr Davis and are believed to have been originally discovered by M. [*sic*] Honegger...who conducted several excavations for Sir Thomas Reade.

It is probable that all those stelae that do not come from the above-mentioned collections were acquired by Davis, from different sources and different sites. NPu1 and NPu2, both inscribed, resemble stelae from Algerian sites, such as Guelma and el-Hofra and may come from that region. NPu3–17 (and possibly NPu18), form a group, carved in precise geometrical style with inscriptions within raised rectangular frames. Characteristic of this group are the standards, somewhere between a caduceus and a stylised tree, often with circles on the shafts; a Tanit symbol is also usually depicted. The names on the inscriptions are Numidian, Latin (written in that language or in neo-Punic) and Punic. The dedications to the deity, where they still exist, are to Baal or Baal Hammon, with no mention of Tanit. These are probably among the stelae excavated by Honegger and acquired by Davis from Crow, as it is the only group of inscribed neo-Punic stelae in the collection. In a letter written by Davis from Carthage in 1857 to the Earl of Clarendon (Foreign Office)[9] he writes

> ... I have also great pleasure in informing your Lordship that I have succeeded in procuring a number of Punic antiquities discovered by Mr Honegger who resided in this country and died in London about 1849. A portion of these come from Zama... Another portion comes from Kef... or Sicca Veneria... the remainder come from Baja, the ancient Vacca... Mr Honegger has left no documents... It is impossible to classify these antiquities.

Davis does not say from whom he acquired these antiquities though it is clear from his book that they came from Mr Crow.

There are four stelae of this type from the Reade collection,[10] acquired by the Museum in 1858. This again suggests that they were probably excavated by Honegger whose patron was, as we know, Sir Thomas Reade. Bisi 1967[11] illustrates a stela of similar type, of unknown provenance. Bourgade 1852, *9ième Tunisienne*, illustrates a complete stela of the same type (**see Fig. 3**).

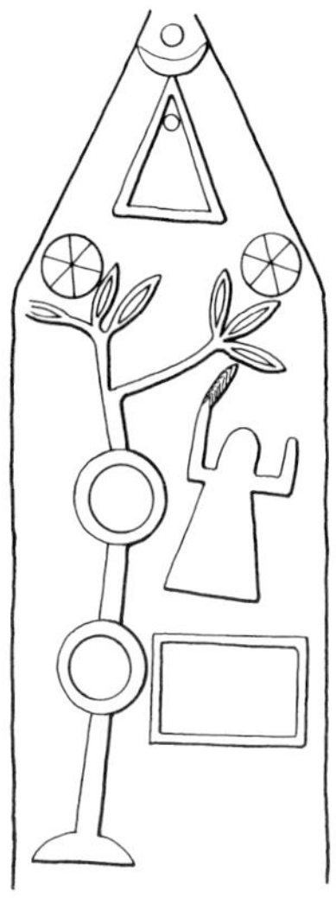

Figure 3 Stela with caduceus/tree/ standard combination and Tanit symbols

Technique

The quality of decoration and of carving varies considerably. There are rare examples of well carved or incised decoration (Pu5, Pu63) while others, in contrast, have hastily scratched designs or inscriptions (Pu59, Pu80). For the most part, though, the carving is competent but uninspired. Incised decoration is common in the Punic period but there are exceptions: in Pu1 the figure in the pediment is in such high relief as to be three-dimensional, Pu5 is very well carved in low, almost flat relief, and Pu24, a small fragment, shows a hand in relief. Pu42 combines incised and relief decoration with some of the relief created by cutting away the background. This is also a feature on Pu10, Pu25 and Pu32. The differences in technique are probably due to different workshops or masons and are not chronological. The inscriptions are always incised, probably by craftsmen other than those who carried out the decoration. There are many examples of misspellings and misjudgments of space.

In the post-Punic period the stelae are carved in relief, usually low and flat, though when a figure is shown standing in a niche it is in high relief. There are strong contrasts in styles. Some stelae continue the Punic tradition, using Punic, non-figurative symbols – if it were not for the neo-Punic inscriptions they could in fact belong to the Punic period. There is a sharp contrast between these and most of the others where human figures predominate, though some symbols are retained.

Most of the stelae, Punic and neo-Punic alike, were 'mass-produced' in workshops and were not made to order. The purchaser would select the one he [or she] wanted and an appropriate inscription would then be added. The decorated stelae are almost always better inscribed than those which only have inscriptions. It may be that only the former were carved by professional masons.

Material

All the stelae except one (the marble plinth Pu72) are from a range of fine-grained limestones (see Appendix 4). Since there is no apparent difference in the material of the Punic, neo-Punic, or even later Roman periods, it is likely that the same quarries were used. Pu73, once thought to be a red sandstone, is actually a fine-grained limestone. A very few stelae (NPu21, Pu74) appear to have been treated in some way, probably by the application of wax as a preservative during the last century.

Stela function

Most of the stelae from the Carthage and other tophets were votive monuments, placed there to commemorate a dedication to a deity or deities in fulfilment of a vow. Beneath the stela were placed one or more urns containing the cremated bones of children and/or animals which many scholars assume were sacrificed. Some of the stelae in the collection are funerary in character [though not those from the tophet]; this is usually clear from the inscription. Some time during the neo-Punic period it is possible that a change occurred and that the stela itself replaced the urn and its contents as the dedication. This is the case in NPu21, from Maktar, which is dedicated to Baal Hammon by the citizens of that city. Usually the purpose of the stela is obvious from its style but it can happen that, as in NPu3-17, where the stelae were acquired already decorated, votive and funerary stelae are indistinguishable except for the inscription. NPu 11 and 13 have inscriptions which are probably funerary but the decoration is identical to the others in the group. It seems that the products of at least one workshop were multi-purpose.

Punic and neo-Punic

One of the more obvious ways of distinguishing between uninscribed Punic and neo-Punic stelae is size. Stelae of the later Punic period (4th-2nd centuries BC) are fairly small, averaging around 13.5 cm in width, while those of the neo-Punic period are much larger, averaging around 31 cm in width.[12] The decoration of the earlier stelae from Carthage tends to be incised rather than in relief while that of the later period is always in relief.

The evidence seems to indicate an overlap between the two distinct styles which may have begun in the 2nd century BC and continued for some time. The stelae belonging to this intermediate group, of which there are two in this collection, NPu1 and NPu2, are larger than the earlier stelae but smaller than those considered neo-Punic. These two, as mentioned earlier, are stylistically similar to stelae from el-Hofra (Constantine) and Guelma which have produced both Punic and neo-Punic inscriptions. The iconography is purely Punic, generally depicting a Tanit symbol, a caduceus or a standard. In other words, Roman influence has not yet taken hold.

Distinct iconographic changes occur on neo-Punic stelae which make the differences between Punic and neo-Punic clear cut and point up the transitional nature of the others. There is a marked decline in the use of inscriptions though they do still occur on tombstones. Human figures are depicted in the neo-Punic period – a feature very rare earlier. The crescent moon, common in both periods, usually has its ends pointing down and enclosing a disc in the Punic period; the opposite is the case later on when the ends always point up and the disc when not shown on its own appears with a rayed sun or a face. The raised hand, palm facing out disappears completely while the caduceus, so common earlier, changes into a standard. The Tanit symbol gradually evolves into a nude female figure and appears with symbols of Classical mythology. It is possible that some differences are due to a change in the function of the stelae: for example, some of the more elaborate may have come from a temple rather than a tophet and the stela might have been the offering rather than an indication of one.

Inscriptions

The inscriptions of the Punic period are almost all the standard dedicatory type which begin, 'To the lady to Tanit face of Baal and to the Lord to Baal Hammon', though in many cases the beginning has been lost. Pu15 has a cursory inscription, 'which vowed Arish'. Pu59 simply has a letter *taw*, possibly for Tanit. Pu1 differs in this as it does in other details, introducing itself as *NṢB MLK B'L* (stela of MLK B'L). The meaning of MLK B'L is obscure though it is thought to indicate a type of sacrifice. The inscription, and the unusual iconography which shows a human figure in the apex carved almost in the round, sets it apart from the others.

On the whole there does not seem to be any connection between iconography and inscription. This may seem obvious if it is agreed that most of the stelae were acquired ready-made from workshops. There are some stelae, however, though not in this catalogue, where the decoration may indicate the occupation of the dedicant. These were probably made to order.

Other non-standard inscriptions are Pu72 – Pu75. Pu72 is a plinth, not a stela, with a slightly ambiguous inscription. Pu73 is part of a dedication plaque set in the wall of a temple or sanctuary. Pu74 is an offering list very similar to that known as the 'Marseilles Tariff' and Pu75 may be part of an altar step.

Only one neo-Punic stela, NPu21, has a firm provenance. The inscription states clearly that it was dedicated to Baal Hammon by the citizens of Maktar. It was found by Sir Grenville Temple at Maktar/Maghrawa in 1833.

Maktar and Maghrawa are two sites faily close to each other. Temple writes that he found the stela at Maghrawa (see Appendix 3) though the inscription is clear that it comes from Maktar. He may have known Maktar as Maghrawa or just possibly the stela may have been brought to Maghrawa at some point from whence he acquired it.

As the Phoenician alphabet did not have vowels the reconstructions of the names are not always certain. The transliterations given here are based on previous transcriptions, on Hebrew parallels, on traditional renderings and sometimes based on the Latin forms. For example, for names composed with MLQRT, it is probable that the Phoenician form was Milqart though it has been traditionally transliterated as Melqart. The same is true of the use of TNT which traditionally is Tanit but is now thought to have been pronounced Tinnit. On the transliteration and translation of the inscriptions we have for the most part restored letters where possible when the letters were all on the stone but are damaged. When the part of the stone which contained the inscription is completely gone we have not restored.

Provenance of the neo-Punic stelae

A number of attempts have been made to discover the true provenance of the type of stela – our NPu24-42 – said by some to come from the Ghorfa,[13] in central Tunisia. One theory[14] suggests that they were found in the 'village' of Ghorfa between 1860 and 1873 by prince Mohamed and Mustapha Khaznadar. Transported to Tunis via Thugga, one stela was said to have accidentally been left there. This led to the idea[15] that they had been excavated at Thugga. The stelae were said to have been in the Musée du Khaznadar de la Manouba from whence they were eventually dispersed, one group purporting to have gone to the British Museum.[16] The latter is a myth; the neo-Punic stelae were already in the Museum by 1860. Obviously they could not have been found between 1860 and 1873.

Another, more recent, suggestion[17] has been that stelae of this type come from Maghrawa near Maktar and were found by J.B. Honegger, who is known to have excavated there in the 1840's.[18] They are thought to have been found by him in 1842 and transported to Tunis in two stages, being deposited first at Thugga from whence a large number were later taken to Tunis by Nathan Davis (and presumably are then supposed to have gone to the British Museum). The remainder went to other collections, including that of Khaznadar. Aside from the fact that similarities between the so-called 'Ghorfa' stelae and those from Maghrawa are superficial, all the 'Ghorfa' stelae in the British Museum came via Nathan Davis and there is no suggestion by him that any of them come from either Maghrawa or Maktar. The evidence in the Museum archives, however, does suggest that they were excavated by Honegger.[19] Our 'Ghorfa' stelae are so similar to those in the Khaznadar collection that they must have the same provenance.

We thus have two distinct groups of neo-Punic stelae without provenance, one group mainly inscribed (NPu3-17 and perhaps 18), the other mainly not. (NPu1 and 2 are a separate group.) We also have three sites of the late Punic and neo-Punic period said (by Nathan Davis) to have been explored by Honegger – Zama, Le Kef, and Sicca Veneria – the stelae from which were acquired by Davis and sent to the Museum. It is therefore likely that the so-called 'Ghorfa' stelae come from one of these places.

The inscribed group, probably also excavated by Honegger at one of the above-mentioned sites, comes from a tophet, though at least two inscriptions appear to be funerary. The symbolism and the language follow Punic tradition and show little sign of Roman influence apart from the occasional Latin name. The 'Ghorfa' stelae appear to be much later and only rarely have a short neo-Punic inscription of dedication. These may come from a temple.

The 'Ghorfa' provenance seems to have originated in an article by Louis Poinssot published in Paris in 1905.[20] In that article he wrote that in around 1863 a company of soldiers of the Khaznadar, accompanied by two Englishmen, came from Maktar to Thugga carrying a large number of 'Roman stones'. The locals who had carried the 'stones' indicated that they had originated in the Ghorfa. Two stelae from this group were registered in the Louvre in 1876 with the mention (according to Poinssot) that they were sent by General Khereddine, provenance, doubtful, la Ghorfa.

The Ghorfa provenance, in spite of the doubts in the Louvre register, was accepted by many scholars writing on the subject. No one thought to explain how the 18 or 19 stelae of this type came into the British Museum before 1860, at least three years before they were supposed to have been found.

Correspondence with the Museum by a Tunisian archaeologist, A. M'charek, who was looking for information about the so-called 'Honegger Collection', sent this author into the Museum's archives where the correspondence in Appendices 1 and 2 was eventually found. It seems, therefore, that M'charek is correct in thinking that the so-called Ghorfa stelae were excavated by Honegger but probably is wrong in thinking they come from the site he has excavated, Maghrawa.

Notes

1 In 1863 a group of ninety inscribed stelae were published by W.S.W. Vaux in a volume entitled, *Inscriptions in the Phoenician Character now in the British Museum Discovered on the Site of Carthage during Researches made by Nathan Davis Esq. at the Expense of Her Majesty's Government in the years 1856, 1857 and 1858* (BMPI).

2 Davis 1861, 434f.

3 See Appendix 2.

4 On whom see below.

5 In 1875, excavations by E. de Sainte-Marie between the hill of St Louis and the sea also produced many stelae. (See E. de Sainte-Marie, *Mission à Carthage* (Paris 1884), ll. 39).

6 Davis 1861, 59, 444ff.

7 More recent British excavations at Carthage have also uncovered stelae from the tophet re-used in a Roman wall, on the 'îlot de l'Amirauté', the circular naval harbour used by both the Carthaginians and the Romans. See *The Antiquaries Journal*, LV (1975), 38-9, Appendix I by V. Wilson, and pl. X.

8 Kelsey 1926

9 See Appendix 2.

10 NPu3, NPu16, NPu17, NPu18

11 Fig. 91.

12 Width, rather than height measurements have been given because so many stelae are incomplete.

13 The Ghorfa is geographically part of the High Tell, situated midway between Thugga and Maktar. It is scarce in ancient sites and is not mentioned in the archaeological atlas of Tunisia nor in any modern tourist guide.

14 Alaoui 1954, 262

15 Alaoui 1897, 62-3.

16 Alaoui 1897, 62.

17 Jongeling, 1984.xviii-xix; M'charek 1988, 747-9;

18 Honegger offered a collection of antiquities which he wrote came from Maghrawa/Maktar to the British Museum in 1848 (see Appendix 1) but the sale was never finalised, probably due to his death in 1849. We do not know what happened to the objects he offered though it is clear from the descriptions he gives that they are not in the British Museum.

19 See Appendix 2.

20 L. Poinssot, Les stèles de la Ghorfa, *Bulletin Archéologique du Comité des Travaux Historiques et Scientifiques*, (1905), 395-407.

Iconography

Tophet stelae of the first centuries of Phoenician settlement in the western Mediterranean often show a symbol or a stylised human figure in a niche. At Carthage, from the 4th century BC, when the material used changes from sandstone to limestone, the stelae begin to exhibit Hellenistic influence – apart from a marked reluctance to portray the human figure, a reluctance which continues until well into the neo-Punic period. Though human figures are not totally absent (they occur on tomb markers), they are comparatively rare. The Phoenicians clearly preferred to express their religious beliefs by the use of symbols, some of which are still not clearly understood.

The iconography of the later stelae is more varied than in the Punic period, partly because provenances are more varied and partly because of their greater chronological range, which covers a period not far short of 500 years, from the end of the 2nd century BC to the 3rd or possibly the beginning of the 4th century AD. (The stelae of the Punic period in the collection cover only around 200 years, from the 4th to the 2nd century BC.) Probably the most important reason for the greater variety, however, is the addition of cultures other than Punic. Numidian and then Roman iconographic ideas combine with the Punic to produce a cultural amalgamation which is uniquely North African.

Punic period (4th-2nd centuries BC)

Tomb Markers

The eight tomb markers in the collection are typical of those found at Carthage. No stelae of this type have been found in the tophet and they are not thought to be votive but funerary in character. They were placed, at Carthage, above family tomb groups to indicate the site, perhaps for the purpose of ceremonial libations to the dead. They are fairly plain, without any inscription, with most of the surface left rough apart from the centre. They all show a figure standing in a niche, possibly a deity, in a long unadorned garment. The right arm is raised in blessing or prayer while the left hand is bent inwards to the waist and holds an offering. TM8 is more elaborate and, with its fluted columns and capitals, shows Hellenistic influence. The main characteristic of the markers is that the raised right hand is often disproportionately large.[1] This is in keeping with the hand raised in blessing or prayer which is so popular on the votive stelae from the tophet.

Tophet Stelae

Compared to the many thousands of stelae from the Carthage tophet which have now been found and are in collections all over the world, the British Museum collection is small. All are from the later Punic period (Tanit III- 400-146 BC); many are fragments with only the inscription or a bit of decoration remaining. There is therefore a limited iconographic range and not surprisingly the symbols used are, on the whole, those most commonly found in the tophet. The most popular are a Tanit and a hand or hand and arm, sometimes shown together, sometimes separately. A caduceus appears on 20 stelae, a combined caduceus/Tanit three times. Standards appear three, perhaps four times without a Tanit and the same number with the symbol on it. Flowers are shown on 15 stelae, though a recognisable palmette appears only once.[2] Rosettes are depicted five times.

The main motifs are the following:

Animals. Animals are uncommon. A fish and ostrich appear once each, and sheep are shown twice. They are usually found in the space normally used for the dedication inscription and may illustrate the offering given.

Architectural motifs. Architectural motifs appear on many stelae, all showing Hellenistic influence. They include bead and reel, dentil, ovolo and egg and dart mouldings, usually placed just below the apex. The other features of note are columns which appear with Ionic capitals on two stelae only, one of them a tomb marker, meant to depict a rudimentary shrine or niche. These features, except for the columns, may be purely decorative and not have any ritual meaning.

Baetyl. A baetyl, or bottle idol, as it is sometimes called, appears only once, in the apex, on an altar. It is not as rare in other collections and it is more common on the sandstone stelae from earlier periods of the tophet and at other sites such as Sousse. Baetyls are also depicted on pendants and scarab seals of the 8th-6th centuries BC found at Carthage and other sites in the western Mediterranean where it is the central votive feature, shown either on its own or with Egyptianizing uraei. In the later Punic period they are hardly ever found.

Caduceus. (**Fig. 4**) A caduceus consists of three basic elements, a shaft with two circles for the finial, the lower one closed, the upper one almost always open. There are many variations: it may have a base or streamers, be shown in a double or single outline, the shaft may be straight or may taper. It is also shown combined with other motifs. It appears on 22 stelae, on three occasions combined with a Tanit symbol. On Pu53 it is combined with both a Tanit and a palm tree.

Probably derived from the symbol of the Greek god Hermes, albeit usually without the wings and snakes, the caduceus is common on the later stelae. For the Greeks and Etruscans it was associated with Hermes as guide of the

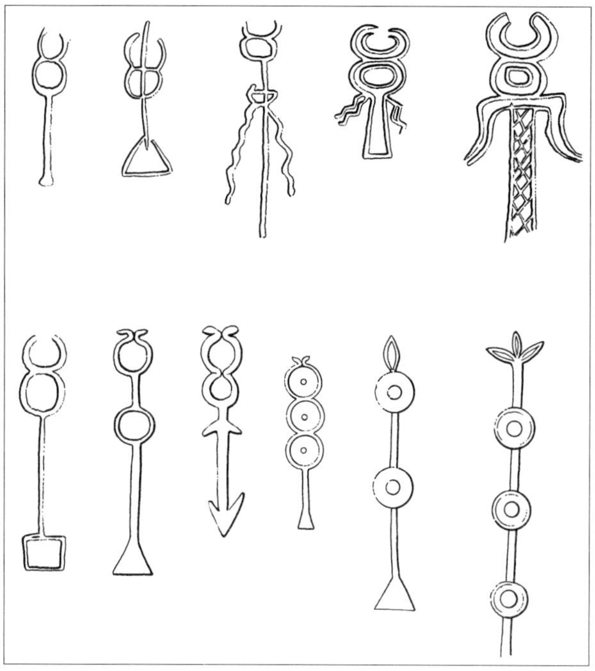

Figure 4 Development of the caduceus

dead to the underworld and this would seem to be appropriate for its appearance on the stelae. If this were so, however, it would mean that the caduceus should only appear on stelae connected to human remains and, unfortunately, we cannot connect the contents of the urns with the stelae. The caduceus also appears on stelae which depict sacrificial animals.[3] It may be that it had a different meaning for the Phoenicians, who perhaps used the symbol of Hermes as a way of conveying their message to the deity.

Crescent and Disc. The crescent and disc (as a single symbol) is probably the most Near Eastern motif to be found, rivalled only by the rosette and the sun. It is known in Mesopotamia as early as the end of the 3rd millennium BC and is common both there and in Syria and the Levant from the 2nd millennium BC on. It occurs here only eight times, probably because of the randomness of the collection and the fragmentary nature of many stelae. The crescent ends point down encompassing the disc. The crescent, symbolizing the new moon, does not appear here without a disc, though it does occur elsewhere either alone, enclosing a rosette or, rarely, with ends up enclosing a rayed sun.[4] The disc probably signifies the full moon, not the sun, though it is possible that the meaning changed under Hellenistic and Roman influence and the full moon became the sun in the neo-Punic period.[5] It rarely appears in the later period where it is sometimes replaced by a wreathed or rayed sun face or a rosette, both of which are shown above a crescent with its ends facing up. Unlike on stelae of the neo-Punic period and those from el-Hofra[6] there does not seem to be any special association with the Tanit symbol.

Flowers, stylised. (See also Lotus.) Though there is only one palmette in its basic form most of the stylised flowers on six stelae may be palmettes. They appear in the apex of the stela and all but two have volutes. All show Hellenistic influence. The palmette appears on Punic pottery, jewellery and seals and is part of the earlier eastern Phoenician repertoire.

Hand. A hand or hand and arm appears on twenty-three stelae, usually in the apex. It is invariably shown as a right hand, palm outward, raised either in blessing or prayer, it is impossible to tell which. On one stela, Pu21, the hand has only four fingers, perhaps carelessness by the mason but more probably done deliberately. Together with the crescent and disc the hand is one of the more obvious iconographic symbols with a Near Eastern origin, found on many different types of object, from seals to stelae throughout the Levant and Mesopotamia. A votive stela from a Late Bronze Age temple at Hazor shows two raised hands below a crescent and disc. There, however, it is clear that the hands are praying, though some archaeologists have seen these hands as a forerunner of the Hebrew priestly benediction.

Humans. There is only one stela with a human/divine figure though another shows a crude head and two more show, respectively, a foot and eyes. This shows a standing robed figure, perhaps female, holding what may be an *ankh* in its left hand with the right hand raised in the usual gesture. The inscription on this stela, Pu1, is unusual, and there may be a connection between the depicting of the human figure and the object it is holding and the inscription which speaks of a type of sacrifice.

Lotus. Lotus flowers appear on ten stelae, usually below the inscription but occasionally in the apex. The number of petals varies: generally three but sometimes, as on Pu63, five. The lotus was very popular on Phoenician objects and appears on ivories and metal bowls as well as on seals. It is one of many Egyptian symbols adopted by the Phoenicians and given its own character. While its function may be decorative on other objects, or even when appearing as part of the stela architecture, there is clearly some ritual significance in the fact that it appears in the body of the stelae, along with more obviously votive symbols such as the 'Tanit', caduceus and hand.

Standard. Standards are usually shown in pairs, either supporting a Tanit symbol or on their own, flanking another symbol. On Pu59 a single standard consists of a shaft on a square base with a circular finial, looking like a heavily pruned bay tree. The stela on which it appears is unusual in that there is no inscription and only the standard, a triangle and a *taw* are shown. The meaning of the standard is uncertain and the way it is shown on Pu59 suggests a link between them. It is usually distinct from a caduceus and the two appear together. At some point during the later stages of the Punic period, probably during the 2nd century BC, a fusion seems to have taken place and it may be that to the Punic mind the two symbols became interchangeable. This is even more apparent in the neo-Punic period when the caduceus rarely appears but a standard with caduceus characteristics is often depicted. (see below, p.000 (np standards)).

Sun. A rayed sun appears only once, on Pu40, along with a crescent and disc and a raised hand and arm.

Tanit. The Tanit symbol in its basic form consists of a triangle or trapezoid, a circle and a horizontal line. The horizontal line often supports two vertical straight or curved lines which can be seen as upraised arms. The symbol may rest on a pedestal (Pu3, Pu4, Pu8 and Pu14) and sometimes has feet (Pu12, Pu13 and Pu14). On Pu5 the centre of the triangle contains a rosette.

The meaning of the Tanit symbol has been much discussed and there are many theories as to its meaning and origins. It first appears at Carthage during the second half of the 5th century BC and until recently has been mainly found in the western Mediterranean. Recent finds in the Levant have provided examples of the symbol and mention of the name as early as the 8th-7th century BC[7] though most of the examples are later, where the name can be combined with that of Astarte.[8] The motif is traditionally known as a Tanit symbol though a definite connection between the symbol and the goddess has not yet been firmly established.[9] A drawing in Euting 1883, pl.198, no.360 (**Fig. 5**), shows a Tanit symbol with a *'taw'* in the triangle. This may indicate a link, but the motif also frequently appears on stelae from el-Hofra[10] which were mostly dedicated to Baal Hammon and where Tanit, when present, is named after Baal.

Any discussion of the meaning of the symbol must also include the neo-Punic and transitional period for it is only thus that its evolution from a geometrical to an anthropomorphic symbol can be clearly seen (**Fig. 6**). The triangle, circle and line (no doubt each with its own meaning) gradually, under classical influence, evolved into the form of a human female figure. On stelae of the Roman period she is depicted as a figure of fertility and abundance and was probably amalgamated with Juno/Caelestis.

Early Tanit symbols closely resemble the Egyptian *ankh*, a symbol of life. Some of the Phoenician female figures found in the sea or on the Phoenician coast of a pregnant goddess or goddess and child also have an ankh or a Tanit symbol.[11]

Figure 5 Tanit symbol with a 'taw'

Figure 6 Development of the Tanit symbol

Wavy line. This feature is shown four times on our stelae. Its meaning is obscure but it may have some connection with water and the sea.

Wreaths. Wreaths appear on four stelae only. On three they act as a register divider below the apex and on one of these there is a rosette in the centre. The wreath on Pu22 may be a symbol of victory.

The neo-Punic period (2nd century BC – 3rd century AD)
Many stelae from the 1st century AD onwards show a human figure in a niche or shrine, either the dedicant if the stela is votive or the deceased if it is a tombstone. Many hold an offering and stand by an altar. On NPu33 a small Victory figure holds aloft a wreath. This type usually has three registers with the niche in the middle. At the top are deities and/or their symbols and below there may be a sacrificial scene or, rarely, a short inscription.

The iconography is rich and varied and some of the symbols used are still unexplained. This is not unexpected when one bears in mind that at least two different cultures, Roman and Numidian, were added to a Punic core. Hellenism also left its mark, as it did on the earlier stelae. The depiction of cult objects is comparatively rare and, when it does occur, may mean that the dedicant was a priest or priestess and these were 'the tools of the trade'. Altars often appear, either in the shrine with the dedicant or else above it next to a Venus figure.

Some of the symbols which were common earlier continue to be used. These include the Tanit, the standard/caduceus, the crescent moon and the rosette. The hand, so popular previously, totally disappears. The disc which formerly always appeared with the crescent also disappears and is sometimes replaced by a wreathed face (the sun) or a rosette (?a star) above, not below, the crescent. Both the Tanit and the caduceus evolve, the Tanit becoming a female figure and the caduceus turning into a standard. New symbols of Roman cults also appear.

Common symbols:
Basket. (see also Casket, Cista). Baskets, caskets or *cistae* are shown on eight stelae. On NPu46 and NPu52 the basket holds an offering, probably incense, which is being placed on an altar by the dedicant. They seem to be ordinary containers without ritual significance. However, the gabled baskets which are depicted on very late Roman stelae dedicated to Saturn do appear to have some religious meaning for they are either carried on the heads of servants or priests during a bull sacrifice or else rest on the floor by the side of the person performing the ritual.

Birds. There are birds on 17 stelae, the cock and the eagle being the most distinctive. The cock was probably a sacrificial animal as on NPu19, while the eagle was a divine symbol. NPu18 shows a bird, probably a dove, flanked by winged Victories holding palm frond and wreath. Birds sometimes appear in the pediment of the shrine in which the dedicant stands. On NPu33 they peck at a human face, on NPu36 and NPu49 there is an eagle, and on NPu36 a cock. On many stelae they appear in the field, usually pecking at fruit. According to Goodenough the birds feeding on grapes symbolise the devotee obtaining[12] divine life.

Bull sacrifice. Eight stelae show scenes of bulls being sacrificed. Four of these are very late, after the 2nd century AD, on stelae dedicated to Saturn, and probably come from a temple. NPu46 is also a dedication to Saturn but is earlier and is in a different, more classical, style. Of the others, NPu45 is on a stela dedicated to Jupiter though Leglay[13] thinks that the two deities are here amalgamated. NPu43 shows the bull being killed with a spear while in the background a musician plays the twin pipes of Cybele. It is unlikely that this is a dedication to Saturn as that ritual was usually carried out with an axe. (For a fuller discussion of this unusual scene see the catalogue entry.) NPu24 shows a bull being killed with a knife.

Caduceus/Standard. Though the caduceus is popular on stelae of the Punic period, it rarely appears in the neo-Punic period in a recognisable form although the standard (see below) acquires some of its characteristics, especially the circles. It is likely that its original symbolism (perhaps as a symbol of healing) has changed and that for some reason, perhaps because of the similar shape, it fused with and was replaced by the standard. A recognisable caduceus appears on only two stelae, NPu2 and NPu49.

Casket. Caskets with gabled lids appear on the latest stelae, either carried on the head or held in the hands as a container for an offering. NPu61 shows a large gabled casket on the floor beside a dedicant. These stelae are all dedications to Saturn, as is NPu51 where the casket is one of a group of cult objects shown with a head of Saturn. The casket may be a container for offerings or it may hold ritual objects.

Cista. *Cistae* are cylindrical vessels, often of wickerwork, which were sometimes used as containers for ritual objects. As such they appear on NPu23 and NPu24 where they are placed within a pedestal with other votive objects, on NPu23 a juglet, unidentifiable on NPu24, but possibly a libation vessel and a ritual hammer or *malleus*, two objects used in Roman sacrificial ritual.

Cornucopiae. Cornucopiae are powerful symbols of abundance and fertility. They appear on nine stelae, always held by a Tanit figure in an upper register. Emerging from them are fruit clusters (dates or grapes) and pomegranates.

Crescent. A crescent appears on 13 stelae but only once with a disc, a change from the earlier periods. The single disc occurs on NPu2, which belongs to the transitional period – probably the 2nd century BC – where it is part of a Tanit symbol consisting of a triangle, crescent and disc, the crescent being the arms and the disc, the head. In another change from the Punic period, the crescent ends always point upwards on neo-Punic stelae. The crescent invariably appears with a Tanit symbol, sometimes as part of the figure, sometimes above it. On NPu41 and NPu42 it appears above an anthropomorphic Tanit as a horned head with a rayed head (sun). Elsewhere it appears with a rosette or a wreathed sun face. On NPu32 the rosette is in a raised disc.

The evidence thus seems to indicate a link between the crescent moon and Tanit in the neo-Punic period. At el-Hofra there is also sometimes an association between the Tanit symbol and the crescent moon.[14]

Cupid. A winged Cupid appears on three stelae, always with Dionysus and Venus. On NPu41 he stands in the pediment of the shrine holding fig or vine leaves. On NPu31 and NPu32 he stands on the pediment where he holds the *thyrsus* of Dionysus in his right hand and with his left extends a wreath over the altar of Venus.

Dionysus and Venus. These deities appear together, though sometimes, due to the fragmentary nature of the stela, only one remains. They are shown on the pediment of the shrine containing the dedicant, one on each side. Venus usually has an altar by her side, while Dionysus holds a two-handled cup and occasionally a *thyrsus*. Sometimes a Cupid appears on the apex of the pediment with a wreath. The dominant symbol on the stelae on which these deities appear is, however, an anthropomorphic Tanit.

Palm fronds. Palm fronds or branches appear as a symbol of victory when held by a winged Victory figure, but may have a different meaning when shown on their own, usually by the side of a shrine. This occurs on NPu23, NPu45 and NPu48.

Rosettes. Rosettes appear on thirteen stelae, with varying numbers of petals. They can be on a raised disc, enclosed by a circle or have sunken centres. They appear to have an astral significance, and may be associated with a particular star (?Venus). The rosette was a star symbol in the second millennium BC in Syria and Mesopotamia, and is frequently found on Phoenician objects, especially on ivories, bronze bowls and seals. It is associated with a female deity, often Astarte or Ishtar.

Saturn. The cult of Saturn was very popular in North Africa and a number of temples to the deity have been discovered. He appears on eight stelae, of which four are very late, dating to the 3rd – 4th centuries AD. He is usually shown with the Dioscuri though they are missing on NPu51 and NPu52. On NPu45 Jupiter is perhaps combined with Saturn and stands on a pedestal with a thunderbolt and an eagle.

Standard. By the neo-Punic period the caduceus had virtually disappeared and seems to have been replaced by a standard, which is often depicted with the circles characteristic of a caduceus. Unlike the caduceus it usually appears in pairs, either flanking a Tanit symbol or on either side of a niche. On the transitional NPu2 it is a true combined standard/caduceus, with an arrow-like shaft. It may have leafy finials or, as on NPu21, be completely tree-like. On NPu44 the finials are spear-shaped. Its most frequent appearance is on the 'geometric' group NPu3–NPu17, but it is also common on the so-called 'Ghorfa' group. On NPu28, it supports a winged Victory figure in an echo of its function as a Tanit support during the Punic period. Like the caduceus in the Punic period, the standard was popular on stelae of the neo-Punic period, appearing in its varying forms on twenty stelae.

Sun. There is a sun on ten stelae, though the raised discs which appear on others may be sun symbols. It is shown as a face with rays or enclosed by a wreath. On NPu41 it is a rayed bust, on NPu42 a face in the pediment with very large rays; on the latter, in addition, there are two heads just below the pediment wreathed by what may be snakes. NPu49, a stela of unusual type, has a wreathed sun from which emerge three running feet.

Tanit. The most common symbol is still that of Tanit, appearing on 27 stelae, sometimes more than once. Her appearance varies more than in the Punic period: on the two transitional stelae, NPu1 and NPu2, she is baetyl-like; on NPu2 there is a second, very imaginative Tanit formed by a triangle, crescent and disc. Another fanciful Tanit is on NPu16 consisting of a triangle and disc with leaves as arms. The symbol becomes increasingly anthropomorphic, first acquiring a head and face, sometimes wreathed, and then taking the form of a nude female holding fruit emerging from cornucopiae. Tanit is usually associated with the crescent moon (see above). However, when there is an inscription on a stela with a Tanit symbol, the only deity named is Baal Hammon.

Victory/Nike. Winged figures, sometimes in pairs, are symbols of victory. They are shown, one holding a palm frond, the other a wreath. On NPu18 they crown a bird, on NPu25 they appear twice, above and below the shrine. On NPu32 a single unwinged figure holding a wreath appears in the niche with the dedicant.

Wreaths. Wreaths appear on fourteen stelae, held by a Cupid, Venus or a Victory figure, worn by Dionysus or Tanit, or used to enclose a sun face (NPu34, NPu40, NPu49). Unusual wreaths on NPu42 enclose sun faces but have no leaves and are in two parts: at the top two ?snake heads face each other while fish-like tails meet below.

****

Circles and holes

It is worth noting a feature which occurs on a number of neo-Punic stelae and which may in some cases have an iconographic meaning. This is the use of drilled sunken or concave circles or of small holes arranged in groups. Holes and circles may have different functions.

Holes

On some stelae, particularly the latest, small holes have been drilled into the stone in groups. Ribbons or streamers may have been inserted into the holes or they may have held an inlay. It is unlikely they had any iconographic significance. NPu25, NPu29, NPu30, NPu37, NPu38, NPu45, NPu49, NPu53, NPu54, NPu55, NPu56

Sunken circles

These sometimes appear on the same stelae as the little holes but may have a different purpose. They are countersunk with an inner, deeper circle. These also occur in groups often in the field but sometimes in architectural features such as architraves and capitals. They may have held an inlay but probably had some iconographic meaning. NPu24, NPu25, NPu26, NPu29, NPu33, NPu35, NPu40, NPu41, NPu42

Large sunken circles

Two stelae have large sunken circles. On NPu27 there are three in the pediment. Two large circles occur on NPu12, one of the 'geometric group', flanking a Tanit symbol. Clearly this type of circle has a symbolic meaning, probably astral.

Concave discs

Another type of sunken circle is shown on some stelae: a concave disc with a raised boss in the centre. These appear mainly on the shafts of standards but on two stelae, NPu11 ('geometric' group) and NPu44, two are in the field, and appear to have an astral meaning. On NPu28 there are two in the pediment, together with other astral symbols, but here they have long handles and seem to be libation vessels.

On standards: NPu3 ('geometric' group), NPu25 ('Ghorfa' group), NPu26 ('Ghorfa' group), NPu28 ('Ghorfa' group), NPu44.

Other kinds of circle are also shown, on standard shafts and in the field. They may be flat with slightly sunken centres, or plain discs.

NPu52, a Saturn stela, has three symbols at the top, next to a head of the god. They are a *falx*, a *cista* and two raised circles with incised central circles.

The concave discs with central bosses are similar to the *phalerae* worn by soldiers on Roman monuments. These are thought to be military awards or service medals. It is possible that this type of disc on the stelae also has a military connection although they are not being worn. The plain or slightly concave discs on standards may also have a military significance, being somewhat similar to the *armillae* on Roman monuments. These were worn by soldiers who had won them for deeds of special merit.

Notes

1 Brown 1991, 136, strongly suggests that these images are human, not divine. However, it is unlikely that they represent an individual as it is thought that they are markers for family, not individual, tombs.
2 Stylised flowers, particularly those with volutes, may be meant to be palmettes but are so highly stylised that they cannot be included.
3 See Brown 1991, figs. 27-31.
4 See Picard, *Karthago* XVIII (1978), pl. XVI.2.
5 The appearance of a rayed sun with a crescent and disc on Pu40 certainly suggests that it is indeed the full moon.
6 Bertrandy-Sznycer 1987, 62-3.
7 Sader 1991. The more recent excavatioons (June 1997) of part of the cemetery from which these objects came has produced additional stelae, one of which also has a Tanit symbol. See A. Badawi in *National Museum News,* no. 6 (London 1997), 37
8 F. Bertrandy, 'Les représentations du signe de Tanit sur les stèles votives de Constantine... in *RSF XX*,1 (1993), 3-28, provides an up-to-date summary of most of the theories, the discoveries in the Levant of the symbol and of the name though she omits the most recent, for which see Sader 1991.
9 It is rare to find *tnt* as part of a personal name. Ashtart, Baal, Melqart and Eshmun are the most common at Carthage.
10 Bertrandy-Sznycer 1987, 55
11 Most of these figures are in private collections but one has been published in E. Gubel *et al, Les Phéniciens et le monde Méditerranéen* (Brussels 1986), 124, no. 55
12 Goodenough 1954, IV, 37-8.
13 Leglay 1961, 225.
14 See discussion of the Tanit symbol in the Punic period above.

Index of Iconographic Symbols

Symbols on Punic Stelae

Altar/offering table (1)
Pu27 = 125284

Ankh? (1)
Pu1 = 125091

Baetyl/bottle (1)
Pu60 = 125305

Caduceus (20)
Pu 6 = 125261
Pu6a = 118787
Pu25 = 125232
Pu27 = 125284
Pu35 = 125248
Pu42 = 125089
Pu44 = 125247
Pu45 = 125233
Pu48 = 125291
Pu49 = 125280
Pu50 = 125272
Pu51 = 125238
Pu52 = 125237
Pu54 = 125223
Pu55 = 125234
Pu56 = 125249
Pu57 = 125087
Pu58 = 125265
Pu59 = 125300
Pu65 = 125307

Caduceus/Tanit combination (3)
Pu14 = 125323
Pu16 = 135693
Pu52 = 125085

Chevron (1)
Pu69 = 125266

Columns (2)
Pu62 = 125222
TM8 = 125182

Crescent and disc (8)
Pu1 = 125091
Pu6 = 125261
Pu40 = 125304
Pu44 = 125247
Pu45 = 125233
Pu46 = 125269
Pu47 = 125282
Pu51 = 125238

Disc and crescent (see Crescent and disc)

Egg and dart moulding (8)
Pu 4 = 125084
Pu11 = 125258
Pu35 = 125248
Pu39 = 125088
Pu42 = 125089
Pu55 = 125234
Pu65 = 125307
Pu70 = 125256

Eye (1)
Pu8 = 125279

Fish (1)
Pu43 = 125718

Flowers – lotus/lily (10)
Pu7 = 125293
Pu16 = 135693
Pu23 = 125230
Pu49 = 125280
Pu57 = 125087
Pu63 = 125250
Pu65 = 125307
Pu66 = 125292
Pu67 = 125083
Pu68 = 125719

Flowers – stylised (6)
Pu40 = 125304
Pu42 = 125089
Pu64 = 125227
Pu65 = 125307
Pu66 = 125292
Pu67 = 125083

Foot (1)
Pu41 = 125208

Hand/hand and arm (23)
Pu6a = 118787
Pu 7 = 125293
Pu20 = 125253
Pu21 = 125311
Pu23 = 125230
Pu24 = 125228
Pu25 = 125232
Pu26 = 125216
Pu27 = 125284
Pu28 = 125271
Pu29 = 125286
Pu30 = 125251
Pu31 = 125285
Pu32 = 125277
Pu33 = 125295
Pu34 = 125254
Pu35 = 125248
Pu36 = 125299
Pu37 = 125264
Pu38 = 125287
Pu39 = 125088
Pu40 = 125304
Pu80 = 125298

Humans (1)
Pu1 = 125091

Human head (1)
Pu82 = 125278

Incense shovel? (1)
Pu27 = 125284

Ivy leaf (1)
Pu62 = 125222

Ostrich (1)
Pu5 = 125244

Ovolo moulding (1)
Pu32 = 125277
Pu37 = 125264
Pu38 = 125287
Pu57 = 125087

Palmette (1)
Pu67 = 125083

Palm tree (2)
Pu21 = 125311
Pu42 = 125089

Platform/dais/pedestal (10)
Pu2 = 125252
Pu3 = 125239
Pu4 = 125084
Pu7 = 125293
Pu8 = 125279
Pu10 = 125260
Pu14 = 125323
Pu19 = 125221
Pu59 = 125300
Pu60 = 125305

Pomegranate (1)
Pu36 = 125299

Rosette (5)
Pu5 = 125244
Pu6 = 125261
Pu10 = 125260
Pu11 = 125258
Pu61 = 125289

Sheep (2)
Pu28 = 125271
Pu42 = 125089

Standard (4)
Pu42 = 125089
Pu52 = 125237?
Pu59 = 125300
Pu68 = 125719

Standard with Tanit (3)
Pu21 = 125311
Pu22 = 125267
Pu23 = 125230

Sun/rayed disc (1)
Pu40 = 125304

Tanit (25)
Pu2 = 125252
Pu3 = 125239
Pu4 = 125084
Pu5 = 125244
Pu6 = 125261
Pu6a = 118787
Pu 7 = 125293
Pu 8 = 125279
Pu 9 = 125210
Pu10 = 125260
Pu11 = 125258
Pu12 = 125276
Pu13 = 125209
Pu14 = 125323
Pu15 = 125308
Pu16 = 135693
Pu17 = 125211
Pu18 = 125224
Pu19 = 125221
Pu20 = 125253
Pu21 = 125311
Pu22 = 125267
Pu23 = 125230
Pu28 = 125271
Pu53 = 125085

Triangle (3)
Pu39 = 125088
Pu59 = 125300
Pu62 = 125222

Triglyph and metope (2)
Pu7 = 125293
Pu18 = 125224

Vase (1)
Pu24 = 125228

Wavy line (4)
Pu6 = 125261
Pu17 = 125211
Pu18 = 125224
Pu42 = 125089

?Wheatsheaf (1)
Pu5 = 125244

Wreath (?laurel) (4)
Pu 6 = 125261
Pu22 = 125267
Pu36 = 125299
Pu42 = 125089

Symbols on Neo-Punic Stelae

Altar (19)
NPu19 = 125177
NPu24 = 125043
NPu26 = 125101
NPu30 = 125190
NPu31 = 125186
NPu32 = 125197
NPu33 = 125072
NPu37 = 125184
NPu38 = 125189
NPu43 = 125075
NPu44 = 125185
NPu45 = 125066
NPu46 = 125115
NPu52 = 125116
NPu53 = 125176
NPu54 = 125181
NPu55 = 125077
NPu56 = 125345
NPu57 = 125191

Athena (1)
NPu20 = 125079

Atlas/caryatid figures (7)
NPu45 = 125066
NPu46 = 125115
NPu47 = 125200
NPu52 = 125116
NPu54 = 125181
NPu55 = 125077
NPu56 = 125345

Baetyl (1)
NPu1 = 125056

Basket (see also Casket, Cista) (6)
NPu46 = 125115
NPu52 = 125116
NPu53 = 125176
NPu54 = 125181
NPu55 = 125077
NPu56 = 125345

Birds (17)
NPu18 = 125090
NPu19 = 125177
NPu20 = 125079
NPu25 = 125192
NPu26 = 125101
NPu27 = 125174
NPu28 = 125102
NPu29 = 125183
NPu30 = 125190
NPu32 = 125197
NPu33 = 125072
NPu34 = 125098
NPu35 = 125063
NPu36 = 125021
NPu41 = 125076
NPu45 = 125066
NPu49 = 125180

Branches (other than palm) (3)
NPu31 = 125186
NPu48 = 125178
NPu49 = 125180

Breastplate (1)
NPu49 = 125180

Bucranium (1)
NPu1 = 125056

Bull (12)
NPu24 = 125043
NPu34 = 125098
NPu41 = 125076
NPu43 = 125075
NPu45 = 125066
NPu46 = 125115
NPu47 = 125200
NPu49 = 125180
NPu53 = 125176
NPu54 = 125181
NPu55 = 125077
NPu56 = 125345

Caduceus (see also standards) (2)
NPu2 = 125117
NPu49 = 125180

Caryatids (see Atlas/Caryatid)

Casket (2)
NPu52 = 125116
NPu53 = 125176

Circles (18)
NPu3 = 125100
NPu11 = 125057
NPu12 = 125118
NPu19 = 125177
NPu22 = 125070
NPu24 = 125043
NPu25 = 125192
NPu26 = 125101
NPu27 = 125174
NPu28 = 125102
NPu29 = 125183
NPu33 = 125072
NPu35 = 125063
NPu40 = 125078
NPu41 = 125076
NPu42 = 125062
NPu44 = 125185
NPu52 = 125116

Cista (3)
NPu23 = 125073
NPu24 = 125043
NPu52 = 125116

Cock (3)
NPu19 = 125177
NPu35 = 125063
NPu36 = 125021

Cornucopia (13)
NPu25 = 125192
NPu28 = 125102
NPu29 = 125183
NPu30 = 125190
NPu31 = 125186
NPu33 = 125072
NPu34 = 125098
NPu35 = 125063
NPu36 = =125021
NPu37 = 125184
NPu40 = 125078
NPu41 = 125076
NPu52 = 125116

Crescent (13)
NPu2 = 125117
NPu25 = 125192
NPu26 = 125101
NPu27 = 125174
NPu28 = 125102
NPu29 = 125183
NPu30 = 125190
NPu31 = 125186
NPu34 = 125098
NPu35 = 125063
NPu36 = 125021
NPu40 = 125078
NPu41 = 125076

Crescent and disc
NPu2 = 125117 (1)

Cup/bowl (7)
NPu19 = 125177
NPu20 = 125079
NPu23 = 125073
NPu30 = 125190
NPu31 = 125186
NPu32 = 125197
NPu45 = 125066

Cupid (3)
NPu31 = 125186
NPu32 = 125197
NPu41 = 125076

Dionysus (8)
NPu24 = 125043
NPu30 = 125190
NPu31 = 125186
NPu32 = 125197
NPu33 = 125072
NPu37 = 125184
NPu38 = 125189
NPu41 = 125076

Dioscuri (6)
NPu45 = 125066
NPu46 = 125115
NPu53 = 125176
NPu54 = 125181
NPu55 = 125077
NPu56 = 125345

Disc (4)
NPu2 = 125117
NPu16 = 125103
NPu34 = 125098
NPu45 = 125066

Dolphin (2)
NPu19 = 125177
NPu42 = 125062

Eagle (2)
NPu35 = 125063
NPu49 = 125180

Falx (5)
NPu46 = 125115
NPu52 = 125116
NPu53 = 125176
NPu55 = 125077
NPu56 = 125345

Fleur-de-lis (1)
NPu44 = 125185

Flower (5)
NPu30 = 125190
NPu33 = 125072
NPu40 = 125078
NPu41 = 125076
NPu49 = 125180

Goat (1)
NPu49 = 125180

Grape/date clusters (15)
NPu25 = 125192
NPu26 = 125101
NPu27 = 125174
NPu28 = 125102
NPu29 = 125183
NPu30 = 125190
NPu31 = 125186
NPu33 = 125072
NPu34 = 125098
NPu35 = 125063
NPu36 = 125021
NPu37 = 125184

NPu38 = 125189
NPu42 = 125062
NPu57 = 125191

Horned head (2)
NPu41 = 125076
NPu42 = 125062

Jupiter (1)
NPu45 = 125066

Juglet/*Amphoriskos* (1)
NPu23 = 125073

Leaves (6)
NPu16 = 125103
NPu17 = 136681
NPu25 = 125192
NPu28 = 125102
NPu30 = 125190
NPu48 = 125178

Libation bowl (2)
NPu28 = 125102
NPu44 = 125185?

Lion attacking bull (1)
NPu39 = 125104

Musical instruments (1)
NPu43 = 125075

Palm frond (7)
NPu18 = 125090
NPu23 = 125073
NPu26 = 125101
NPu28 = 125102
NPu45 = 125066
NPu47 = 125200
NPu48 = 125178

Palm tree (2)
NPu34 = 125098
NPu42 = 125062

Pedestal (7)
NPu4 = 125069
NPu10 = 125045
NPu11 = 125057
NPu14 = 125981
NPu24 = 125043
NPu29 = 125183
NPu32 = 125197

Pomegranate (11)
NPu25 = 125192
NPu26 = 125101
NPu27 = 125174
NPu28 = 125102
NPu29 = 125183
NPu30 = 125190
NPu31 = 125186
NPu33 = 125072
NPu34 = 125098
NPu35 = 125063
NPu36 = 125021

Rosettes (13)
NPu2 = 125117
NPu10 = 125045
NPu20 = 125079
NPu27 = 125174
NPu29 = 125183
NPu30 = 125190
NPu35 = 125063
NPu36 = 125021
NPu38 = 125189
NPu41 = 125076
NPu45 = 125066
NPu49 = 125180
NPu57 = 125191

Saturn (8)
NPu20 = 125079
NPu43 = 125075
NPu46 = 125115
NPu51 = 125106
NPu53 = 125176
NPu54 = 125181
NPu55 = 125077
NPu56 = 125345

Scroll (2)
NPu50 = 125179
NPu51 = 125106

Shell (1)
NPu20 = 125079

Snake (1)
NPu42 = 125062

Standards
(see also Caduceus) (20)
NPu2 = 125117
NPu3 = 125100
NPu4 = 125069
NPu5 = 125195
NPu6 = 125105
NPu7 = 125196
NPu8 = 125050
NPu9 = 125194
NPu10 = 125045
NPu11 = 125057
NPu13 = 125198
NPu16 = 125103
NPu17 = 136681
NPu19 = 125177
NPu21 = 125044
NPu25 = 125192
NPu26 = 125101
NPu27 = 125174
NPu28 = 125102
NPu29 = 125183

Sun (wreathed or rayed) (10)
NPu21 = 125044
NPu28 = 125102
NPu29 = 125183
NPu30 = 125190
NPu31 = 125186
NPu34 = 125098
NPu40 = 125078
NPu41 = 125076
NPu42 = 125062
NPu49 = 125180

Table (1)
NPu19 = 125177

Tabula ansata (1)
NPu12 = 125118

Tanit (27)
NPu1 = 125056
NPu2 = 125117
NPu3 = 125100
NPu4 = 125069
NPu5 = 125195
NPu6 = 125105
NPu7 = 125196
NPu8 = 125050
NPu9 = 125194
NPu12 = 125118
NPu16 = 125103
NPu25 = 125192
NPu26 = 125101
NPu27 = 125174
NPu28 = 125102
NPu29 = 125183
NPu30 = 125190
NPu31 = 125186
NPu33 = 125072
NPu34 = 125098
NPu35 = 125063
NPu36 = 125021
NPu37 = 125184
NPu38 = 125189
NPu40 = 125078
NPu41 = 125076
NPu42 = 125062

Thunderbolt (1)
NPu45 = 125066

Thyrsus (5)
NPu20 = 125079
NPu31 = 125186
NPu32 = 125197
NPu33 = 125072
NPu41 = 125076

Tree (see also Palm tree) (6)
NPu4 = 125069
NPu5 = 125195
NPu6 = 125105
NPu13 = 125198
NPu40 = 125078
NPu49 = 125180

Triangle (2)
NPu2 = 125117
NPu16 = 125103

Triquetra (1)
NPu49 = 125180

Vase (1)
NPu23 = 125073

Venus (9)
NPu24 = 125043
NPu30 = 125190
NPu31 = 125186
NPu32 = 125197
NPu33 = 125072
NPu37 = 125184
NPu38 = 125189
NPu40 = 125078
NPu41 = 125076

Vine leaf (1)
NPu41 = 125076

Vulture (1)
NPu33 = 125072

Wheatsheaf (1)
NPu48 = 125178

Winged figures
(see also Cupid) (4)
NPu16 = 125103
NPu18 = 125090
NPu26 = 125101
NPu28 = 125102

Wreath (14)
NPu18 = 125090
NPu26 = 125101
NPu28 = 125102
NPu30 = 125190
NPu31 = 125186
NPu32 = 125197
NPu33 = 125072
NPu34 = 125098
NPu37 = 125184
NPu38 = 125189
NPu40 = 125078
NPu41 = 125076
NPu42 = 125062
NPu49 = 125180

Figure 7 Symbols on Punic stelae

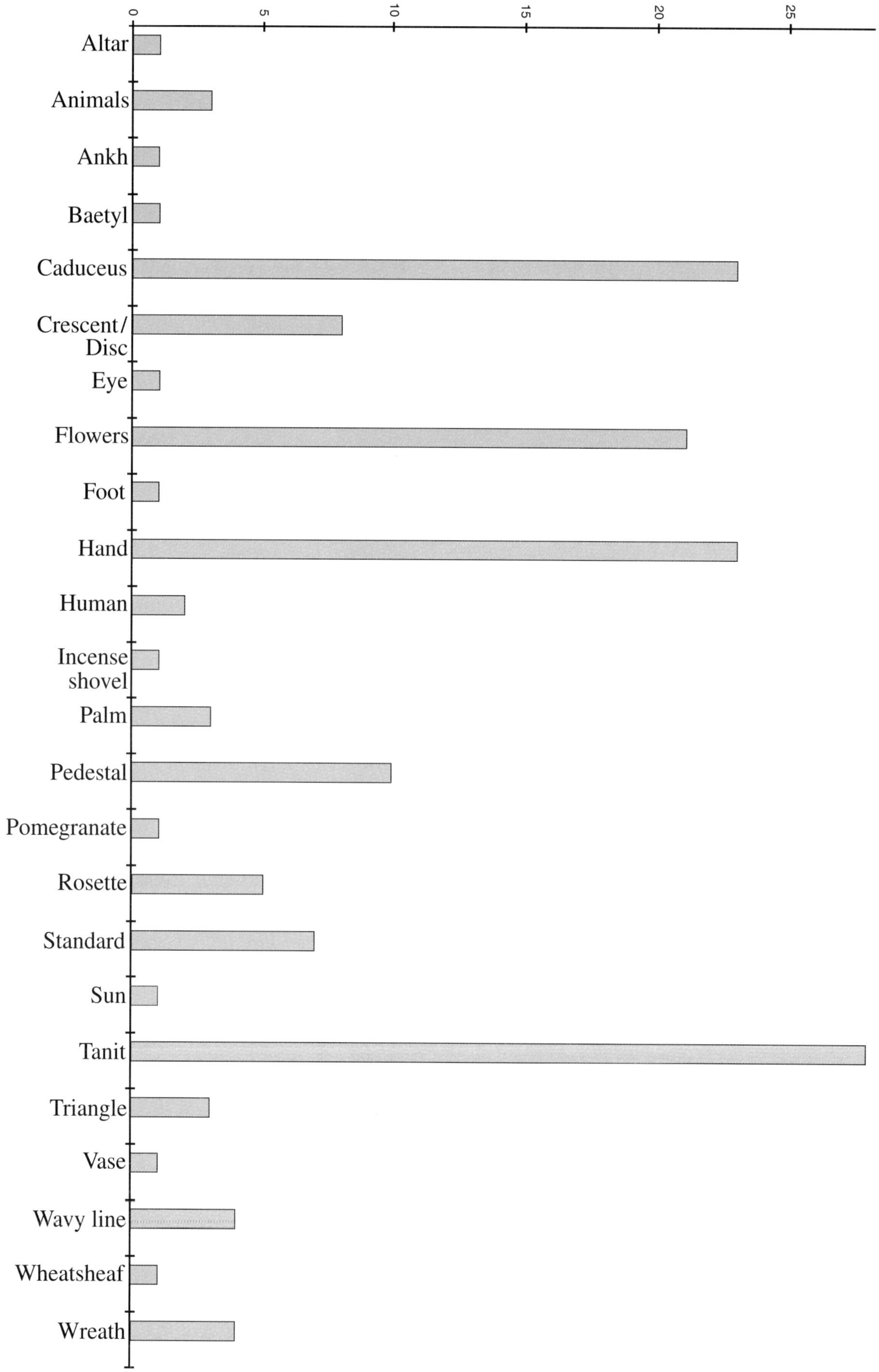

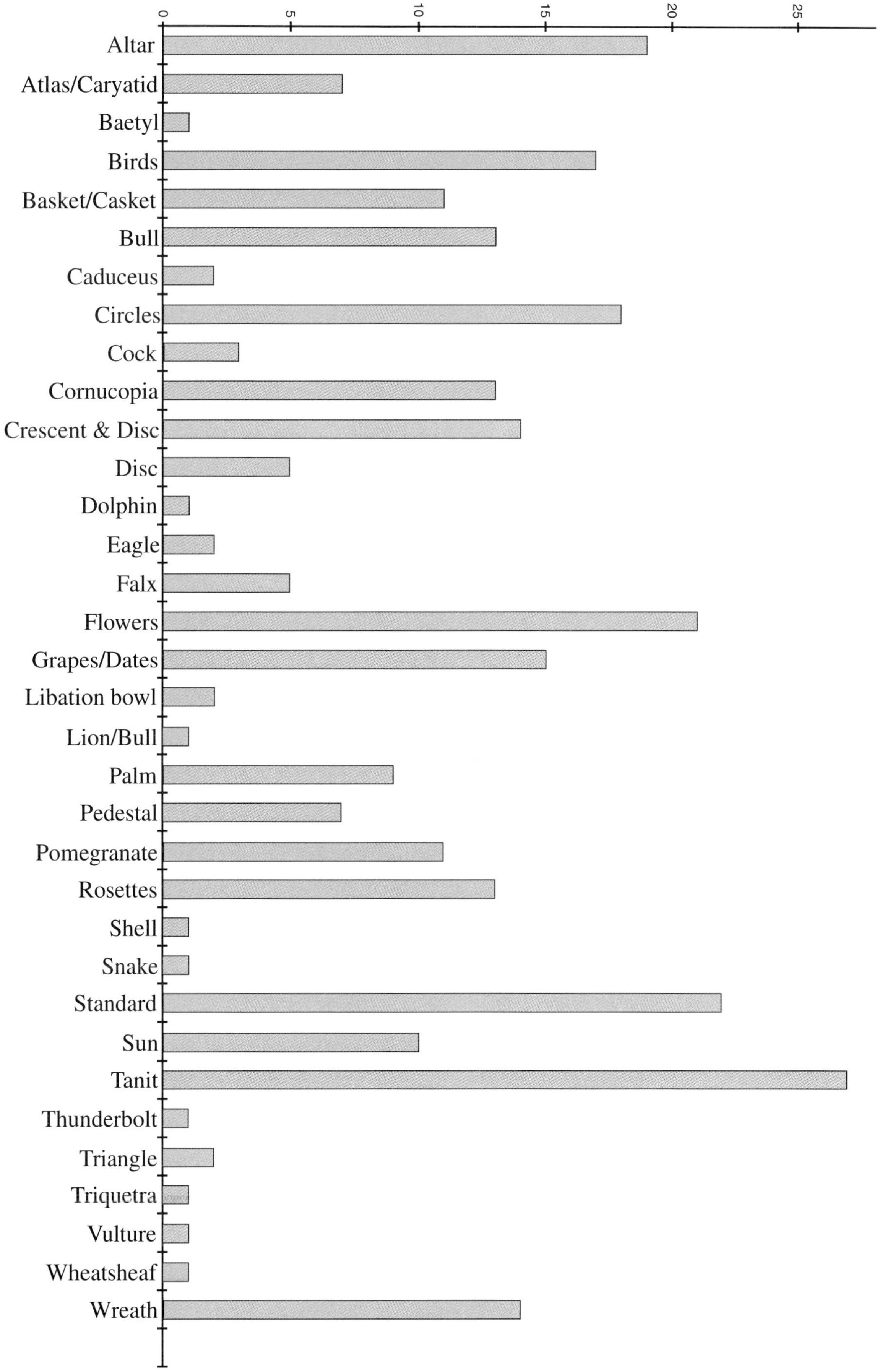

Figure 8 Symbols on neo-Punic stelae

Catalogue

The stelae have been grouped as follows:

1) Tomb markers from Carthage (4th–2nd centuries BC). These were placed above ground to indicate the site of family burial places. There are eight stelae of this type, identical in style to markers from the Carthage cemeteries of Ard el-Kheraib (4th century BC) and Ste Monique (3rd–2nd centuries BC). None are inscribed and they all depict a figure in a niche with right arm raised, palm outward, in blessing or prayer, carved in very high relief;
2) Stelae from the Carthage tophet (4th–2nd centuries BC);
3) Neo-Punic stelae (1st century BC–2nd century AD), some with inscriptions. The different styles suggest that they come from different parts of North Africa. Some are Punic in style and many show Roman and Numidian influence. The neo-Punic writing is often poor though the decoration can be lively. Some may be funerary, rather than votive monuments; comparable examples have been found *in situ* in temples in central Tunisia, deposited as votive objects. Some may also come from a tophet.
4) Stelae of the later Roman period, mostly dedicated to the cult of Saturn (2nd-3rd centuries AD);
5) Tombstones;
6) In addition, some inscribed stones, mainly Punic, do not fit into any of the above categories and are notable for their unusual shape or inscription. In this group are inscribed monuments which came from a temple or temples possibly connected to a tophet. They are catalogued with the stelae from the tophet.

It is not always possible, especially without an inscription, to distinguish between a tombstone, a votive stela commemorating a sacrifice and a memorial stela commemorating a person. This applies more to stelae of the neo-Punic period than to those of the Punic period.[1] The stelae from the tophet are *not* funerary monuments: they were not erected to commemorate the burial of the child or animal whose bones were placed under them but to commemorate a *sacrifice* made in fulfilment of a vow. Indeed, in the neo-Punic period, the stela itself could be the object deposited in fulfilment of a vow.

The stelae of the Punic period fall into two groups, tomb markers and votive monuments, with the exceptions noted in (6) above. There are eight tomb markers and 115 votive stelae, almost all fragmentary. Pu72 is a plinth with an unusual votive inscription and was probably a statue base. Pu71, also with a votive inscription, is in the shape of a column with niches. In addition there are three non-votive inscribed stones, Pu73, Pu74 and Pu75,[2] which come from a temple or sanctuary. Pu74 is a sacrificial tariff list which is similar to the more complete stela known as the Marseilles tariff.[3] Pu73 is a dedication plaque containing the name of the person who probably donated the building. Pu75 is a two-line inscription recording the renovation and rededication of a place of sacrifice or of the steps of a sacrificial altar. The measurements of the stone suggest that the object could be a step.

Tomb markers

TM1. 125071 (60-10-2, 123)

55.5 x 24.5–22.5 x 8.5 cm

Gabled stela, with a slight downward taper. In a gabled niche stands an androgynous figure, probably female, dressed in a plain long robe with round neck. The right hand, disproportionately large, is raised, palm out, in prayer or blessing. The left hand is bent in at the waist and holds an offering. The remainder of the surface has been left rough.

Cf. (for this and the other tomb markers) Cintas 1976, pl. LXXII.

TM2. 125171 (57-12-18, 74)

25.2 x 14.5-14 x 11 cm

Stela with a flat top, and slight downward taper. In a flat-topped niche stands a female figure dressed in a plain long robe with a little V-neck. She wears a necklace with pendants, possibly amulets. Her right hand is raised, palm outward; the left arm is bent in at the waist and holds an offering. The remainder of the surface has been left rough.

TM3. 125187 (57-12-18, 70)

38.2 x 23.5-22.5 x 10 cm

Gabled stela with a downward taper. In a niche with a flat top stands a veiled woman wearing a plain long robe with a round neck. Her right hand is raised, palm out; the left hand is bent in at the waist and holds a bowl. The remainder of the surface has been left rough.

TM4. 125188 (57-12-18, 71)

32.8 x 21-18.5 x 8.5 cm

Gabled stela with a pronounced downward taper. In a gabled niche stands a ?female figure wearing a long robe with a round neck. Her right hand is raised, palm out; the left arm is bent in at the waist and holds an offering. The remainder of the surface has been left rough.

TM5. 125199 (57-12-18, 73)

29 x 23-21.2 x 7.5 cm

Gabled stela with downward taper. In a flat-topped niche stands a ?female figure wearing a plain long robe with a round neck. The large right hand is raised, palm out; the left arm is bent in at the waist and holds an offering. A narrow border around the niche has been smoothed but the remainder of the surface is rough.

TM6. 125319 (57-12-18, 69)

30 x 33 x 10 cm

Stela with flat top, probably originally gabled. In a flat-topped niche stands a female figure wearing a plain long robe. Her head is tilted slightly to the left and the hair is dressed in rows of short curls. The large right hand is raised, palm out; the left arm is bent in at the waist and in her hand she holds an offering, possibly a pomegranate. The remainder of the surface has been slightly smoothed.

TM7. 125317 (57-12-18, 72)

30 x 28.5-26 x 8 cm

Stela with pronounced downward taper. It has a rounded top but was probably originally gabled. In a flat- topped niche stands a female figure. She wears a flounced and pleated robe which leaves her right arm and shoulder bare but covers the left shoulder and arm. Her right hand is raised, palm out; the left is bent in at the waist and holds an offering. The hair shows signs of an attempt to depict curls. The remainder of the surface has been smoothed.

TM8. 125182 (57-12-18, 68)

39.5 x 36 x 10.8 cm

Stela with flat top. In an elaborately carved niche stands a veiled female figure wearing a long robe and sandals. The folds of her clothing are carefully shown and she wears a belt around her hips. The hair is parted in the centre and falls in curls to the ears. The disproportionately large right hand is raised, palm outward; the left arm is bent in at the waist and holds an offering. The niche has elaborately scrolled capitals on either side. The remainder of the surface shows chisel-marks.

Punic Stelae

Pu1. 125091 (S.O.C. 102)

23.4 x 16.9 x 7.3 cm

Stela with sharply pointed apex and acroteria. A female figure in high relief stands in the apex, right hand raised. In her left hand she holds a circle on a t-shaped stem which resembles an ankh or possibly a Tanit symbol. In the acroteria are incised discs and inverted crescents. Below, a band of egg and dart moulding separates the design from a three-line inscription in a plain line frame:

1. *NṢB MLK B'L 'Š NDR MT*
2. *N'LM BN ŠṢP LRBT LTNT PN*
3. *[B'L WL'DN] LB'L[Ḥ]MN KŠM' QL'*

1) Stela of MLK B'L which vowed Mutt 2) unelim son of Shasaf to the lady to Tanit face 3) [of Baal and to the lord] to Baal Hammon for hearing his voice.

This stela has some features which distinguish it from most of the other tophet stelae. The inscription differs in that the dedication to the deity does not come at the beginning. Instead we have the formula, 'Stela of MLK B'L...' which is thought to be to a type of sacrifice, though of what kind is a matter of some discussion. Three (or possibly four) other inscriptions with the same introduction are known, from Malta, Sardinia and Carthage, at least one of which is thought to date to the 7th-6th century BC.[4]

The object in the left hand of the figure is almost unique. However, the discovery at Tyre of engraved stelae and burial urns has produced a stela with an identical symbol.[5]

From the Fenner Coll.6; formerly belonging to G. Wood
Euting 1871, 200; CIS I,1 194; Mendleson 1995, 259-60 and fig. 5
Cf. Hours-Miédan 1951, pl. XXXVc and p. 64 (the disc and crescent are thought to be eyes); Bisi 1967, fig. 31, pp. 74-5, where the figure is said to be holding a lotus flower or vase; CIS I,1, 123, 147, 380. Other figures with offerings are shown in CIS I,2, 989 (a lily), 2863 (a juglet); CIS I,3, pl. XXX.2 shows a nude child with an offering between two squatting figures while no. 8 on the same plate shows a figure holding a flower.

Pu2. 125252 (86-6-21, 6)

25 x 11 x 6 cm

Well-made gabled stela with acroteria. Finely smoothed surface. In the apex is a Tanit symbol on a very narrow pedestal. Below is a five-line inscription:

1. *LRBT LTNT PN B'L W*
2. *L'DN LB'L ḤMN 'Š ND*
3. *R ḤMLKT BN BDMLQR*
4. *T BN 'ZRB'L KŠM'[6] Q*
5. *[L]'*

1) To the lady to Tanit face of Baal and 2) to the lord to Baal Hammon which vow 3) ed Himilkot son of Bodmelqar 4) t son of 'Azrubaal for hearing 5) his voice.

Wright 1886, no. 1; CIS I,2, 2108

Pu3. 125239 (57-12-18, 3)

23 x 10 x 10 cm

Sharply gabled stela with acroteria. In the apex is a Tanit symbol on a pedestal. The head of the Tanit is more hemispherical than circular and the upraised arms are curved. Almost complete five-line inscription:

1. *LRBT LTNT P*
2. *N B'L WL'DN L*
3. *B'L ḤMN 'Š N*
4. *DR MGN[7] BN ḤN'*
5. *[B]N MGN*

1) To the lady to Tanit fa 2) ce of Baal and to the lord to 3) Baal Hammon which vo 4) wed Magon son of Hanno 5) son of Magon.

BMPI pl. 2,4; Euting 1883, 22; CIS I,2, 448

Pu4. 125084 (60-10-2, 3)

24.5 x 12 x 10.2 cm

Gabled stela with Tanit symbol on a pedestal in the apex. The head is almost hemispherical. Below it is a band of angular v-shaped egg and dart moulding. Beneath are three lines of an inscription:

1. *LRBT LTNT PN*
2. *[B]'L WL'DN LB*
3. *['L Ḥ]MN 'Š ND...*

1) To the lady to Tanit face of 2) Baal and to the lord to B 3) aal Hammon which vowed...

BMPI, pl 27,76; Euting 1883, 94; CIS I,2 512

Pu5. 125244 + 125245 (57-12-18, 77, 82)

27.6 x 16.6 x 9.5 cm

Upper part of a well-carved gabled stela with decoration in low relief. No inscription. In the apex is a Tanit symbol on a narrow pedestal with an eight-petalled rosette in the triangle. Below a moulded lintel which separates the pediment from the body of the stela is an ostrich passant to the left, eating from an upright bundle, possibly a wheatsheaf.

Mendleson 1995, p. 260 and fig. 6
Cf. Hours-Miédan 1951, pls. xxiih, xxiva.

P6. 125261 (57-12-18, 30)

25.5 x 14.5 x 5.5 cm

Well-made stela with small gable and acroteria. In the apex is a crescent and disc, the crescent with ends pointing down. In the acroteria are volutes. Below this is a horizontal wreath with six-petalled rosette in the centre. In the centre is a three-line inscription and below that, separated by a plain incised horizontal line, is a Tanit symbol between two caducei. The Tanit stands on a wavy line.

1. *LRBT LTNT P'N[8] B'L WL'*
2. *DN LB'L ḤMN 'Š NDR[9] '*
3. *MTMLQRT BT[10]*

1) To the lady to Tanit face of Baal and to the lo 2) rd to Baal Hammon which vowed A 3) motmelqart daughter of...

BMPI pl. 1,2; Euting 1883, 20; CIS I,2, 446.

P6a. 118787 (1927-9-22, 1)

17.5 x 18.2 x 4 cm

Tapering stela fragment, uninscribed. Deeply incised detail of a Tanit symbol flanked by a hand and a caduceus. The Tanit symbol is incised with double lines except for an elongated lozenge at the tip of the triangle just below the crossbar. At the ends of the crossbar are two curved 'arms'. There is a curved 'headdress' above the circle, identical to the finial of the caduceus beside it. The caduceus has a tree-like shaft incised less deeply and with only a single line, spreading at the base; the raised right hand has elongated fingers; the arm is incised with single lines. The background of the hand is cut away to give an impression of relief as is to some extent the caduceus. Both the hand and caduceus lean outward at a slight angle, parallel with the taper of the stone. Above these symbols is a band of bead and reel.

The Tanit symbol has some unusual features, especially in the use of a caduceus finial with snakes' heads. The elongated lozenge is also unusual. It has been suggested[11] that it is meant to be either male or female genitalia. On this figure it could be either.

Pu7. 125293 (60-10-2, 1)

25 x 14 x 6.5 cm

Gabled stela with voluted acroteria. In the pediment a Tanit symbol stands on a pedestal of triglyphs and metopes. Below this is a band of ovolo moulding; below this is a four-line inscription. Below the inscription is a lotus flower flanked by open right hands and arms.

1. *LRBT LTNT PN B'L WL*
2. *'DN LB'L ḤMN 'Š NDR*
3. *'RŠM BN BD'ŠTRT BN*
4. *BD'ŠMN KŠM' QL' BR[K']*

1) To the lady to Tanit face of Baal and to the 2) lord to Baal Hammon which vowed 3) Arisham son of Bod'ashtart son of 4) Bodeshmun for he heard his voice and blessed him.

Davis 1861, opp. p. 256; BMPI pls. 21, 75; CIS I,2, 511; R.D. Barnett, *Illustrations of Old Testament History*, 2nd edn, (London 1977) 36.

Pu8. 125279 (57-12-18, 25)

18.5 x 12 x 8 cm

Top part of sharply gabled stela with two lines of inscription remaining. In the apex is a Tanit symbol on a pedestal. Below and on either side is an eye, with incised pupil and lashes.

Inscription:

1. *LRBT LTNT*
2. *PN B'L WL'DN...*

1) To the lady to Tanit 2) face of Baal and to the lord...

BMPI pl. 1, 29; Euting 1883, 47; CIS I,2, 471

Pu9. 125210 (59-4-2, 9)

16 x 10.5 x 9 cm

Part of gabled stela with incised Tanit symbol in the apex. Three lines of inscription remain:

1. *LRBT LTNT PN*
2. *B'L WL'DN LB*
3. *'L ḤMN 'Š NDR...*

1) To the lady to Tanit face of 2) Baal and to the lord to B 3) aal Hammon which vowed...

BMPI, pl. 9, 25; Euting 1883, 43; CIS I,2, 467.

Pu10. 125260 (57-12-18, 2)

28 x 14.5 x 7.4 cm

Gabled stela with acroteria. There is a six-petalled rosette in relief (created by cutting away the surrounding background) in the apex and an incised Tanit symbol on a rudimentary pedestal below the five-line inscription. The head of the Tanit is almost hemispherical, as in Pu3.

1. *LRBT LTNT PN B'L WL'D*
2. *N LB'L ḤMN 'Š NDR BD*
3. *'ŠTRT BN 'ŠTRTYT*
4. *N B[N ']ŠMNŠMR KŠM'*
5. *QL[']*

1) To the lady to Tanit face of Baal and to the lo 2) rd to Baal Hammon which vowed Bod 3) 'ashtart son of 'Ashtartyat 4) on so[n of E]shmunshamar for he heard 5) his voice.

BMPI pl. 2,5; Euting 1883, 23; CIS I,2, 449

Pu11. 125258 (86-6-21, 1)

28.5 x 17.5 x 9.5 cm

Gabled stela with delicately carved incised decoration and a four-line inscription. In the apex is a twelve-petalled rosette within a circle flanked by Tanit symbols. Below is a row of egg and dart moulding within incised lines.

1. *[LR]BT LTNT PN B'L W[LDN]*
2. *LB'L ḤMN 'Š NDR 'ZR[B']*
3. *L BN 'BD'ŠMN BN*[12] *BD'[BN]*
4. *'BD'ŠMN*

1) [To the l]ady to Tanit face of Baal and 2) to the lord to Baal Hammon which vowed 'Azru[baa] 3) l son of 'Abdeshmun son of Bodo [son of] 4) 'Abdeshmun.

Wright 1886, no. 7; CIS I,1, 288

Pu12. 125276 (57-12-18, 33)

17 x 11.5 x 5.1 cm

Gabled stela with acroteria, a Tanit symbol with curved feet in the apex. Chiselled surface. Five lines of inscription remain:

1. *[LR]BT LTNT PN B['*
2. *L WL] 'DN LB'L Ḥ[M*
3. *N] 'Š NDR ḤN' BN*
4. *'BDMLQRT BN*
5. *BD'Š[T']RT*

1) [To the l]ady to Tanit face of B 2) [aal and to the] lord to Baal Ha[mmo 3) n] which vowed Hanno son of 4) 'Abdmelqart son of 5) Bod'ashtart.

BMPI 1, 3; Euting 1883, 21; CIS I,2, 447

Pu13. 125209 (57-12-18, 27)

14 x 13 x 9 cm

Stela, once gabled with acroteria which are now missing. Above, the remains of a Tanit symbol with curved feet. Four-line inscription:

1. *LRBT LTNT PN B'[L W]*
2. *L'DN LB'L ḤMN ['Š]*
3. *NDR ḤN' BN BD[ML]*
4. *QRT BN MGN*

1) To the lady to Tanit face of Baal and 2) to the lord to Baal Hammon [which] 3) vowed Hanno son of Bod[mel] 4) qart son of Magon.

BMPI, pl. 4, 12; Euting 1883, 30; CIS I,2, 456

Pu14. 125323 (86-6-21, 7)

48 x 16.5 x 10.2 cm

Large gabled stela, almost complete. It has been attacked by salts and the design and inscription are difficult to see. In the apex is a Tanit symbol on a pedestal. Below the inscription is a combined caduceus/Tanit symbol. Four-line inscription:

1 *LRBT LTNT PN B'L W*
2. *L'DN LB'L ḤMN 'Š N*
3. *DR MGN BN 'ZRB'*
4. *L BN 'BD...*

1) To the lady to Tanit face of Baal and 2) to the lord to Baal Hammon whi[ch] vo 3)wed Magon son of 'Azrubaa 4) l son of 'Abd...

Wright 1886, no. 6, p. 212; CIS I,2, 2113

Pu15. 125308 (59-4-2, 7)

27 x 10 x 8.9 cm

Gabled stela. In the damaged apex are the remains of a Tanit symbol. Below is a two-line inscription:

1. *'Š NDR '*
2. *RŠ*

1) Which vowed A 2)rish.

BMPI pl. 12, 34; Euting 1883, 52; CIS I,1, 425

Pu16. 135693 (60-10-2, 14)

14.5 x 10 x 6.2 cm

Fragment. Part of two lines of inscription remain, below which is the upper part of a combined caduceus/Tanit with upraised curved arms flanked by flowers. Inscription:

1. *...ḤN' BN M*
2. *...[M]HRB'L*

1) ...Hanno son of M 2) ...[M]aharbaal.

BMPI pl. 31, 89; Euting 1883, 107; CIS I,2, 523

Pu17. 125211 (60-10-2, 7)

17 x 13.7 x 7 cm

Fragment with incised decoration and five lines of inscription with a wavy line above and a vertical zig-zag line remaining on one side (the other side is damaged). Above are traces of an unrecognisable symbol and below is the top of a Tanit with upraised curved arms. Inscription:

1. *[LRB]T LTNT PN B'L W*
2. *[L'DN] LB'L ḤMN 'Š*
3. *[ND]R 'BDMLQRT*
4. *[BN] BDMLQRT BN 'B*
5. *[DMLQ]RT KŠM' QL'*

1) [To the la]dy to Tanit face of Baal and 2) [to the lord] to Baal Hammon which 3) [vow]ed 'Abdmelqart 4) [son of] Bodmelqart son of 'Ab 5) dmelqart for he heard his voice.

Davis 1861, opp. p. 256; BMPI, pls. 29, 80; Euting 1883, 98; CIS I,2, 516

Pu18. 125224 (86-6-21, 4)

20.5 x 15.5 x 4.5 cm

Gabled fragment with acroteria. In the apex is the lower part of a Tanit symbol. Below this is a band of triglyph and metope. Below that and with an incised line above and below is a three-line inscription:

1. *[LR]BT LTNT PN B'L WL'*
2. *DN LB'L ḤMN 'Š NDR MG[N]*
3. *[B]N B'LḤN' BN ḤMLKT*

1) To the la]dy to Tanit face of Baal and to the lo 2) rd to Baal Hammon which vowed Mag[on] 3) son of Baalhanno son of Himilkot.

Below the inscription is a double wavy line.

Wright 1886, no. 4; CIS I,2, 2111

Pu19. 125221 (59-4-2, 23)

16 x 9.8 x 3.7 cm

Stela, originally gabled, with a six-line inscription. Above, in the remains of the apex, is the bottom of a Tanit symbol on a narrow base.

1. *[L]RBT LTNT*
2. *PN B'L WL'*
3. *DN LB'L Ḥ*
4. *MN 'Š NDR*
5. *Y/ZKNŠLM*[13] *BN*
6. *'BD'*

1) To the lady to Tanit 2) face of Baal and to the Lo 3) rd to Baal Ha 4) mmon which vowed 5) Y/Zakonshalim son of 6) 'Abdo.

BMPI, pls. 15, 45; Euting 1883, 63; CIS I,2, 484

Pu20. 125253 (76-2-25, 3)

21 x 9 x 5 cm

Gabled stela with acroteria, one missing. Roughened surface, decoration incised. In the apex is an open right hand. Incised lines above and below frame the four-line inscription of which only the beginnings of the lines remain. Below the inscription is the top of a Tanit symbol.

1. *LRBT LTNT...*
2. *[B]'L WL'DN LB...*
3. *'Š NDR BD...*

4. ...BD/R[14] *‘BD...*

1) To the lady to Tanit... 2) [B]aal and to the lord to B[aal]... 3) which vowed Bod... 4) bd/r ‘Abd...

From the Fenner Collection, 9
Euting 1871, 23 & pl. 28, 228; CIS I,2, 543

Pu21.125311 (60-10-2, 16)
34.9 x 16.2 x 7.2 cm
Gabled stela with acroteria. In the apex is an open right hand and arm, the hand with only four fingers. Below this is a band of bead and reel moulding. The surface below the moulding has been roughened, probably in an attempt to erase an inscription. Below the roughened surface is a palm tree with pendent bunches of dates, flanked by Tanit symbols on standards.

Mendleson 1995, 260 and fig. 7.

Pu22.125267 (57-12-18, 29)
11 x 10.4 x 7.9 cm
Stela fragment with four lines of inscription remaining, the top line almost completely lost. Below is a wreath between two Tanit symbols on standards.

1. ... [WL] ’DN [LB‘L ḤM]
2. N ’Š NDR ‘BD’Š
3. MN BN BD[M]LQRT
4. KŠM’ QL’

1) ... [and to the] lord [to BaalḤm 2) n which vowed ‘Abdesh 3) mun son of Bod[m]elqart 4) for he heard his voice.

BMPI pl. 13, 39; Euting 1883, 57; CIS I,2, 480

Pu23.125230 (57-12-18, 17)
16.5 x 11 x 5.5 cm
Stela fragment. Above, traces of a rudimentary egg and dart pattern. Below the five line inscription is the top of a flower with volutes, flanked by Tanit symbols, probably on standards.

1. [LR]BT LTN[T P]
2. N B‘L WL’D[N LB]
3. ‘L ḤMN ’Š N[DR]
4. LBT BT ‘BD[M]
5. LQR[15]*T BN ‘<B>D*[16]*DM[LK]*

1) To the lady to Tanit fa 2) ce of Baal and to the lor[d to B] 3) aal Hammon which v[owed] 4) Labot daughter of ‘Abdme 5) lqart son of ‘<b>dmi[lk].

BMPI pl. 10, 28 where the ‘r’ in l.1 is still mostly preserved; Euting 1883, 46; CIS I,2, 470

Pu24.125228 (57-12-18, 78)
13 x 13.5 x ?cm
Small fragment of gabled stela with mainly relief decoration. Only the apex remains, with a raised border and a well-carved open right hand in relief. In the palm of the hand is an incised juglet.[17]

Pu25.125232 (57-12-18, 75)
14.5 x 8 x ? cm
Stela fragment. In the apex is an open right hand and arm in semi-relief. Below this is the top of a caduceus or stylised flower. The hand and arm have been carved so that it is level with the body of the stone but a border has been cut around it to give an impression of relief.

Mendleson 1995, 259, and fig. 4.

Pu26.125216 (57-12-18, 79)
9 x 5 x ? cm
Small stela fragment, apex only, with an incised open right hand, palm out.

Pu27.125284 (57-12-18, 80)
21 x 16 x 6.5 cm
Fragment of gabled stela with acroteria, apex only remaining. Above is a right arm with open hand and below it are caducei flanking an offering tray.

Pu28.125271 (76-2-25, 2)
17 x 12-10.5 x 6.2 cm
Tapering gabled stela with acroteria, now missing. Roughened surface. In the apex is an arm the hand of which is missing. Below is a sheep passant to the left with the fleece indicated by incised lines. Below the sheep is the top of a Tanit symbol.

Pu29.125286 (60-10-2, 4)
24 x 11 x 6.2 cm
Gabled stela. In the apex is an arm with open right hand, palm out. Four lines of inscription remain and a fragment of a fifth:

1. [LRB]T LTNT PN B
2. [‘L] WL’DN LB‘L Ḥ
3. MN ’Š NDR ’RŠ
4. BN ‘KBR BN ‘BD‘
5. ...QL’

1) To the lady to Tanit face of B 2) aal and to the lord to Baal Ha 3) mmon which vowed Arish 4) son of ‘Akbor son of ‘Abda 5) ...his voice.

BMPI pl. 28, 78; Euting 1883, 96; CIS I,2, 514 which reconstructs the name as ‘BD ‘[ŠTRT]

Pu30.125251 (59-4-2, 14)
26 x 15 x 9 cm
Gabled stela with acroteria. In the apex is an open right hand and arm. Three-line inscription:

1. LRB[18] *LTNT PN B‘L WL’DN L*
2. B‘L ḤMN ’Š NDR ḤMLKT
3. BN ḤN’ BN PDY

1) To the lady to Tanit face of Baal and to the lord to 2) Baal Hammon which vowed Himilkot 3) son of Hanno son of Pady.

BMPI pl. 17, 50; Euting 1883, 68; CIS I,2, 489

Pu31. 125285 (86-6-21, 2)

21 x 16 x 6.5 cm

Gabled stela with acroteria. Roughened surface. In the apex is a right hand, palm out. Below is a five-line inscription:

1. *LRBT LTNT PN B'L WL'*
2. *DN LB'L ḤMN 'Š NDR*
3. *ḤMLKT BN 'BDMLQRT*
4. *BN 'BD'ŠMN KŠM' QL*
5. *' YBRK'*

1) To the lady to Tanit face of Baal and to the lo 2) rd to Baal Hammon which vowed Himilkot son of 'Abdmelqart 3) son of 'Abdeshmun for he heard his voi 4) ce may he bless him.

Wright 1886, 212, no. 5; Euting 1883, 355; CIS I,2, 2112

Pu32. 125277 (60-10-2, 6)

17 x 13.5 x 4.9 cm

Gabled stela with acroteria. In the apex is an arm, hand missing. The back of the arm has been cut away to create the impression of relief, as on Pu10. Below it is a row of ovolo moulding and below that, within a rectangular frame, is a three-line inscription. The rest of the stela is missing but the top of an unrecognisable symbol is just visible on one side.

1. *LRBT LTNT PN B'L W*
2. *L'DN LB'L ḤMN 'Š NDR'*
3. *'BRKT*[19] *BT YḤW' BN BDM*[20]

1) To the lady to Tanit face of Baal and 2) to the lord to Baal Hammon which vowed 3) Aberkat daughter of Yahua[21] son of BDM.

BMPI, pl. 28, 79; Euting 1883, 97; CIS I,2, 515

Pu33. 125295 (76-2-25, 7)

24 x 15.5-14 x 8.9 cm

Gabled stela with acroteria. Roughened surface. In the pediment is a hand and arm. Four lines of inscription are so lightly carved that the reading of the name is uncertain:

1. *LRBT LTNT PN B'L*
2. *WL'DN LB'L ḤMN '*
3. *Š NDR' YTNT [B]T 'B*
4. *[DM]LK BN 'ZRB'L*

.

Both CIS and Euting read: To the lady to Tanit face of Baal and to the lord to Baal Hammon which vowed Ashtanit daughter of Baalshillek son of 'Azrubaal.' The name can also be read Yatanit.[22] We suggest the following reading:

1) To the lady to Tanit face of Baal 2) and to the lord to Baal Hammon wh 3) ich vowed Yatanit daughter of 'Ab 4) dmilk son of 'Azrubaal.

From the Fenner Collection, 8
Euting 1871, 227; CIS I,2, 542

Pu34. 125254 (57-12-18, 14)

24 x 18 x 6 cm

Stela, originally gabled with acroteria, mostly now missing. Remains of an arm and hand in the apex and the top of a caduceus below the five-line inscription:

1. *[L]RBT LTNT PN B'L WL*
2. *[']DN LB'L ḤMN 'Š N*
3. *[D]R GR'ŠT[R]T BN Ḥ*
4. *[ML]KT BN B'LŠLK BN*
5. *[BD]MLQRT*

1) To the lady to Tanit face of Baal and to the 2) lord to Baal Hammon which vo 3) wed Ger'ashtart son of Hi 4) milkot son of Baalshillek son of 5) [Bod]melqart.

BMPI pl. 19, 55; Euting 1883, 73; CIS I,2, 494

Pu35. 125248 (59-4-2, 16)

25 x 13 x 6 cm

Stela, originally gabled with acroteria, top now missing. Decoration incised. Below the apex is a row of egg and dart moulding. In the centre is a three-line inscription; below are a caduceus and a right hand and arm, palm out.

1. *LRBT LTNT[PN B'L]*
2. *WL'DN LB'L Ḥ[MN 'Š N]*
3. *DR 'MTB'L*[23] *B[T]*

1) To the lady to Tanit [face of Baal] 2) and to the lord to Baal H[ammon which]...[vo] 3) wed Amotbaal daugh[ter]...

BMPI pl. 13, 38; Euting 1883, 56; CIS I,2, 479

Pu36. 125299 (86-6-21, 3)

21.5 x 11 x 6 cm

Stela, originally gabled with acroteria. Traces of a hand and arm in the pediment below which is a double wreath. In the centre is a five-line inscription; two incised lines beneath separate it from a pomegranate below which is a single incised line. The inscription is well carved:

1. *LRBT LTNT PN B'L*
2. *WL'DN LB'L ḤM[N]*
3. *'Š NDR BD'ŠTRT*
4. *BN ḤN' BN 'BD'*
5. *ŠMN KŠM'*[24] *QL'*

1) To the lady to Tanit face of Baal 2) and to the lord to Baal Hammon 3) which vowed Bod'ashtart 4) son of Hanno son of 'Abde 5) shmun for hearing his voice.

Wright 1886, 211, no. 2; CIS I,2, 2109

Pu37. 125264 (57-12-18, 35)

11.5 x 14 x 5.8 cm

Stela fragment. Remains of a hand above, separated from the inscription by a row of ovolo moulding and an incised line. The three-line inscription is set in a plain incised frame.

1. *LRBT LTNT PN B'L WL'D*
2. *N LB'L ḤMN 'Š NDR ḤM*
3. *LKT BN BDMLQR[T]*

1) To the lady to Tanit 2) face of Baal and to the lo 2) rd to Baal Hammon which vowed Him 3) ilkot son of Bodmelqart.

BMPI pl. 24, 67; Euting 1883, 85; CIS I,2, 505

Pu38. 125287 (76-2-25, 6)
21 x 16 x 7.9 cm
Gabled stela fragment, originally with acroteria. In the apex are the remains of an arm and hand; below this is a row of ovolo moulding and a four-line inscription:

1. LRBT LTNT PN B'L W
2. L'DN LB'L ḤMN 'Š ND
3. R B'LŠLK BN 'BDM[L]
4. [QRT] BN B'LŠLK

1) To the lady to Tanit face of Baal and 2) to the lord to Baal Hammon which vow 3) ed Baalshillek son of 'Abdme[l 4) qart] son of Baalshillek.

From the Fenner Collection, 7
Euting 1871, pl. 27, 226; Euting 1883, 226; CIS I,2, 541

Pu39. 125088 (57-12-18, 10)
24 x 15-14 x 6.5 cm
Gabled stela with a hand in the apex within a triangular frame. Below is a row of egg and dart moulding. Five-line inscription:

1. [L]RBT LTNT PN B'L
2. [W]L'DN LB'L ḤM[N]
3. 'Š NDR ḤMLKT BN
4. BDMLQRT BN BD'
5. [ŠTR]T

1) To the lady to Tanit face of Baal 2) and to the lord to Baal Hammon 3) which vowed Himilkot son of 4) Bodmelqart son of Bod'a 5) [sht]art.

BMPI, pl. 18, 53; Euting 1883, 88; CIS I,2, 492.

Pu40. 125304 (57-12-18, 24)
23.5 x 12.2 x 6 cm
Gabled stela with acroteria. In the pediment is a stylised flower with volutes. Below is an open hand and arm flanked by a crescent and disc on one side and a disc with rays (star or sun) on the other. Four lines of inscription remain, incomplete with the top of a letter possibly an 'l' on an otherwise missing fifth line:

1. LRBT LTNT PN B'L
2. WL'DN LB'L Ḥ[MN ']
3. Š NDR ḤNB'L ...
4. 'ŠMN...
5. ...L...

1) To the lady to Tanit face of Baal 2) and to the lord to Baal H[ammon wh] 3) ich vowed Hannibaal 4) Eshmun... 5) ...L...

BMPI, pl. 9, 26; Euting 1883, 44; CIS I,2, 468 which reconstructs the end of l. 3 as [BN 'BD] and in l. 4 adds [BN] after the *'ŠMN;* Mendleson 1995, 259, fig. 2.

Pu41. 125208 (86-6-21, 5)
13 x 18 x 5 cm
Gabled stela fragment, originally with acroteria. Incised decoration. In the apex is a foot proceeding right, standing on a horizontal line. Below is a two-line inscription within an incised frame:

1. LRBT LTNT PN B'L WL'DN LB'L ḤMN 'Š
2. NDR 'BD'ŠMN BN MGN

1) To the lady to Tanit face of Baal and to the lord to Baal Hammon which 2) vowed 'Abdeshmun son of Magon.

Wright 1886, 212, no. 3; CIS I,2, 2110

Pu42. 125089 (S.O.C. 100)
40 x 13 x ? cm
Uninscribed stela, with decoration partly in relief and partly incised. Sharply gabled with high acroteria, one missing. In the apex is a stylised floral design in relief. Below it is an ornamental band of bead and reel under which is a horizontal laurel wreath, also in relief. Below this, within a plain incised rectangular frame, is a ram passant to left. At the top of the frame is a wavy line. Below is an incised line with another wavy line beneath, and below this is an elaborate date palm with pendent bunches of dates flanked by combined caduceus/standards/trees, incised and in relief.

Mendleson 1995, 259, fig. 3.

Pu43. 125718 (57-12-18, 4)
19.5 x 13.2 x 10 cm
Stela, top missing. Clearly written four-line inscription below which are two fish facing each other.

1. LRBT LTNT PN B'
2. L WL'DN LB'L ḤM
3. N 'Š NDR ŠPT BN
4. BD'ŠMN BN[25]

1) To the lady to Tanit face of Baa 2) l and to the lord to Baal Hamm 3) on which vowed Shafot son of 4) Bodeshmun son of.

BMPI, pl. 16, 46; Euting 1883, 64; CIS I,2, 485

Pu44. 125247 (57-12-18, 76)
18.5 x 11 x ? cm
Stela fragment, gable only remaining. Incised decoration of, from top to bottom, an inverted crescent, disc with central depression, and the top of a caduceus.

Pu45. 125233 (57-12-18, 83)
16 x 10 x ? cm
Stela fragment, apex only. Incised decoration, from top to bottom, of a caduceus, an inverted crescent, and a disc with a central depression.

Pu46. 125269 (57-12-18, 5)
14.5 x 11.3 x 6.1 cm
Stela with small gable and acroteria, bottom part missing. In the apex is an inverted crescent and a disc. Four-line inscription:

1. LRBT LTNT PN B'L W
2. L'DN LB'L ḤMN 'Š ND
3. R ḤN' BN 'RŠ BN 'Š
4. MNYTN KŠM' QL'

1) To the lady to Tanit face of Baal and 2) to the lord to Baal Hammon which vow 3) ed Hanno son of Arish son of Esh 4) munyaton for hearing his voice.

BMPI pl. 2, 6; Euting 1883, 24; CIS I,2, 450

Pu47. 125282 (59-4-2, 13)

16.4 x 11.7 x 4.5 cm

Gabled stela with acroteria, one side damaged, bottom part missing. In the pediment are traces of a disc and crescent. The three lines of inscription are enclosed top and bottom by a plain incised line:

1. *[LRBT L] TNT PN B'L WL'D*
2. *[N LB'L] ḤMN 'Š NDR 'DR*
3. *[B'L] BN 'ZRB'L BN ḤN*

1) [To the lady to] Tanit face of Baal and to the lor 2) [d to Baal] Hammon which vowed Addir 3) [baal] son of 'Azrubaal son of Han...

BMPI pl. 1, 1; Euting 1883, 19; CIS I,2, 445 which reconstructs [B'L] at the end of line 3 but there is no room at the end of the line for this.

Pu48. 125291 (60-10-2, 2)

23 x 14.5-13 x 10.7 cm

Gabled stela with acroteria. In the apex is a caduceus with streamers. Carelessly written five-line inscription:

1. *LRBT LTNT PN B[']*	
2. *L WL'DN*[26] *LB'L ḤMN*[27]	
3. *[']Š NDR [ḤN] B'L*	3. *CIS: [']Š NDR...B'L*
4. *[B]N 'DNB['L] BN '*	4. *CIS: BN 'DNB'L... '*
5. *KBR*	

1) To the lady to Tanit face of B[aa] 2) l and to the lord to Baal Hammon 3) which vowed [Hanni]baal 4) [s]on of Adonib[aal] son of 'A 5)kbor.

BMPI pl. 27, 74; Euting 1883, 92; CIS I,2, 510 which gives a slightly different reading to BMPI.

Pu49. 125280 (59-4-2, 10)

21.5 x 13.5 x 5.4 cm

Stela with gabled top, a flower and caduceus in the apex. Three lines and a fragment of a fourth line of inscription remain:

1. *LRBT LTNT PN B'L W*
2. *L'DN LB'L ḤMN 'Š*
3. *NDR 'BDMLQRT*
4. *BN M'...*

1) To the lady to Tanit face of Baal and 2) to the lord to Baal Hammon which 3) vowed 'Abdmelqart 4) son of Ma...

BMPI pl. 8, 22; Euting 1883, 40; CIS I,2, 465 which sees l. 4 as BN [*Š '*].

Pu50. 125272 (57-12-18, 1)

18 x 13 x 9.6 cm

Gabled stela with a caduceus on a triangular base in the apex and traces of another symbol at the bottom. Two-line inscription:

1. *LRBT LTNT PN B'L*
2. *WL'DN LB'L ḤM[N]*

1) To the lady to Tanit face of Baal 2) and to the lord to Baal Hammo[n].

BMPI pl. 18, 52; Euting 1883, 70; CIS I,2, 491

Pu51. 125238 (57-12-18, 12)

18.5 x 9 x 10 cm

Gabled stela, point missing. Above are caducei flanking a disc. Below is a six line inscription:

1. *LRBT LTNT*
2. *PN B'L WL'D*
3. *N LB'L ḤMN '[Š]*
4. *NDR BDM[L]QR[T]*
5. *BN B'LYTN BN*
6. *ḤN'*

1) To the lady to Tanit 2) face of Baal and to the Lo 3) rd to Baal Hammon which 4) vowed Bodme[l]qar[t] 5) son of Baalyaton son of 6) Hanno.

BMPI pl. 4, 10; Euting 1883, 28; CIS I,2, 454

Pu52. 125237 (57-12-18, 23)

21 x 15 x 8.5 cm

Gabled stela fragment. Above, is the shaft of a caduceus/standard. Three lines of badly written inscription remain:

1. *[LR]BT LTNT PN B'L L'*
2. *[D]N LB'L ḤMN 'Š NDR*
3. *BD'ŠTRT BN ḤN'*

1) [To the la]dy to Tanit face of Baal (and) to the lo 2) rd to Baal Hammon which vowed 3) Bod'ashtart son of Hanno.

BMPI pl. 5, 13; Euting 1883, 31; CIS I,2, 457

Pu53. 125085 (57-12-18, 8)

22.5 x 14.5 x 8.2 cm

Stela, top and bottom missing, with three lines of inscription remaining, the lower part of the top line only, below which is a combined caduceus/Tanit symbol with a palm-tree shaft.

1. *WL'DN LB'L ḤMN*
2. *'Š NDR BD' BN*
3. *ḤMLKT BN ḤNB'L*

1)...and to the lord to Baal Hammon 2) which vowed Bodo son of 3) Himilkot son of Hannibaal.

BMPI, pl. 7, 20; Euting 1883, 38; CIS I,2, 463

Pu54. 125223 (59-4-2, 24)

12.5 x 11.2 x 6 cm

Stela fragment. Three lines of inscription remain, below which is the top of a caduceus with streamers.

1. *'Š NDR 'ZRB['L]*[28]
2. *BN 'DNB'L BN BD*
3. *MLQRT*

1)...which vowed 'Azrub[aal] 2) son of Adonibaal son of Bod 3) melqart.

BMPI pl. 13, 37; Euting 1883, 55; CIS I,2, 478

Pu55.125234 (59-4-2, 27)

22 x 16 x 10.5 cm

Stela fragment, four lines of a well-written inscription remaining with traces of a band of egg and dart above and a caduceus below.

1. [LRBT LTNT PN]B'L WL'
2. [DN LB'L ḤMN 'Š]NDR 'ZR
3. B'L BN GR'ŠTRT BN BD
4. MLQRT KŠM' QL' TBRK'

1) [To the lady to Tanit face of] Baal and to the L[ord 2) to Baal Hammon which] vowed 'Azru 3) Baal son of Ger'ashtart son of Bod 4) melqart for hearing his voice; may you bless him.

BMPI, pl. 20, 58; Euting 1883, 76; CIS I,2, 497

Pu56.125249 (57-12-18, 20)

27 x 16.5 x 7 cm

Stela fragment, five lines of inscription remaining, below which is the top of a caduceus. Roughened surface.

1. LRBT [LTNT PN B]
2. [']L WL'DN LB['L]
3. ḤMN 'Š NDR' B
4. [T]B'L BT MH
5. RB'L

1) To the lady [to Tanit face of B] 2)aal and to the lord to B[aal] 3)Hammon which vowed Ba 4) [t]baal daughter of Mah 5) arbaal.

BMPI pl. 16, 47; Euting 1883, 65; CIS I,2, 486 (the first name is read as Muttunbaal)

Pu57.125087 (59-4-2, 34; S.O.C.98)

17 x 14 x 6.5 cm

Stela fragment with a five-line inscription within an inset frame. Below is the top of a caduceus and a lily.

1. LRB[T L]TNT PN B'
2. L WL'[D]N LB'L ḤM
3. N 'Š NDR 'ŠMNḤLṢ
4. BN ḤMLKT BN 'ŠM
5. NḤLṢ

1) To the lady to Tanit face of Baa 2) l and to the lord to Baal Hamm 3) on which vowed Eshmunhilles 4) son of Himilkot son of Eshmu 5) nhilles

BMPI pl. 25, 2; Euting 1883, 90; CIS I,2, 509

Pu58.125265 (76-2-25, 1)

8.5 x 11.6 x 3.8 cm

Stela fragment, only one legible line of inscription remaining below which is an incised line. Below the line is the top of a caduceus.

1. [BN 'ŠMN[29]]
2. [N]DR 'BDMLQRT B[N]

1) [...son of Eshmun] 2)...vowed 'Abdmelqart so[n]...'

From the Fenner Collection, 10
CIS I,2, 544; Euting 1871, pl. 28, 229 and p. 23

Pu59.125300 (60-10-2, 17)

25.5 x 9 x 7.2 cm

Gabled stela. In the apex is a triangle and a standard. Below, in the centre, is a large letter taw, possibly for Tanit.[30]

BMPI, pl. 31, 88; Euting 1883, 106; CIS I,1, 396

Pu60.125305 (57-12-18, 13)

26 x 11 x 9.9 cm

Gabled stela with bottle/baetyl on a pedestal in the apex. Below is a four-line inscription:

1. LRBT LTNT PN B[']
2. L WL'DN B'L ḤM
3. N 'Š NDR BDMLQ
4. RT BN 'BD'ŠMN

1) To the lady to Tanit face of Baa 2) l and to the lord Baal Hamm 3) on which vowed Bodmelq 4) art son of 'Abdeshmun.

BMPI, pl. 8, 24; Euting 1883, 42; CIS I,2, 466

Pu61.125289 (60-10-2, 11)

17 x 9.3 – 8 x 7.7 cm

Stela fragment split lengthways resulting in the loss of the first words of each line. The top was probably gabled. Above, two four-petalled rosettes; below, three part-lines of inscription:

1. ...'L WL'DN LB
2. ... B'LYTN
3. ...BN 'S...

1)...[B]aal and to the lord to B 2) [aal Hammon which vowed] Baalyaton 3) ...son of AS...

BMPI pl. 30, 84; Euting 1883, 102; CIS I,2, 519

Pu62.125222 (57-12-18, 81)

25 x 15.2 x 10.7 cm

Stela fragment, originally gabled, no inscription. Smoothed surface. The incised decoration is well carved and depicts a temple facade with columns supporting Ionic capitals. Within the shrine is an ivy leaf within a pediment. Above are traces of a crescent and disc.

Cf. Hours-Miédan 1951, pl. XVIIb and p. 40

Pu63.125250 (76-3-11, 1)

25.5 x 12.1 x 6.4 cm

Lower part of a stela with the last line of an inscription below which is a well-carved lotus flower/water lily.

1. YTN KŠM' [31] *QL' BRK'*

1) Yaton for he heard his voice and blessed him.

From the Fenner Collection, 3
Euting 1871, pl. XIII, 197 and p. 18; CIS I,2, 538; Hours- Miédan 1951, pl. XXIb

Pu64.125227 (57-12-18, 26)

21.5 x 15.2 x 6 cm
Gabled stela fragment with a large stylised flower with volutes in the apex. Below, only one line of inscription remains:

1. LRBT LTNT PN B'L

1) To the lady to Tanit face of Baal

BMPI pl. 15, 44; Euting 1883, 62; CIS I,2, 483 which sees part of a second line W[L...]

Pu65.125307 (57-12-18, 19)

19.5 x 8 x 7.9 cm
Gabled stela with acroteria. In the apex is a stylised flower below which is a band of egg and dart moulding. There is a four-line inscription below which are the remains of a caduceus flanked by lotuses.

1. [L]RBT LTNT PN
2. [B']L WL'DN LB'L
3. ḤMN 'Š NDR' [']
4. RŠT BT B'LY[TN]

1) To the lady to Tanit face of 2) Baal and to the lord to Baal 3) Hammon which vowed [A] 4) rishat daughter of Baalya[ton].

BMPI, pl. 7, 19; Euting 1883, 37; CIS I,2, 462

Pu66.125292 (59-4-2, 12)

24 x 14.5 x 10.7 cm
Gabled stela with acroteria. In the apex is a stylised flower with volutes. Below the four line inscription is part of a lily.

1. LRBT LTNT PN B'L W[L]
2. 'DN LB'L ḤMN 'Š [NDR']
3. ḤTMLKT BT Ḥ [32] *... [M]*
4. GN BN M... [33]

1) To the lady to Tanit face of Baal and [to the] 2) lord to Baal Hammon which [vowed] 3) Hotmilkat daughter of H...[Ma] 4) gon son of M...

BMPI, pl. 14, 41; Euting 1883, 59; CIS I,2, 482

Pu67.125083 (59-4-2, 25)

12 x 15 x 6.1 cm
Inscribed stela fragment with a floral design above, with volutes. Two lines of inscription remain and the tops of the letters of a third:

1. LRBT LTNT PN B'L
2. WL'DN LB'L Ḥ[MN]
3. 'Š [NDR B/G]D/R'ŠTRT

1) To the lady to Tanit face of Baal 2) and to the Lord to Baal Ha[mmon] 3) which [vowed B]od'ashtart (BMPI) or [G]er'ashtart (CIS).

BMPI, pl. 23. 64; Euting 1883, 82; CIS I,2, 503

Pu68.125719 (57-2-18, 7)

18 x 10.5 x 7.1 cm
Stela, top and bottom missing. Well-written six-line inscription, the top line almost completely missing. Below the inscription is the top of a large lotus flower flanked by standards.

1. LRBT [LTNT PN]
2. B'L WL'DN [LB]
3. 'L ḤMN 'Š ND
4. R ḤN' BN BD'
5. ŠTRT BN 'BD
6. MLQRT

1) To the lady [to Tanit face of] 2) Baal and to the lord [to B] 3)aal Hammon which vow 4) ed Hanno son of Bod'a 5) shtart son of 'Abd 6) melqart.

BMPI, pl. 7, 21; Euting 1883, 39; CIS I,2, 464

Pu69.125266 (59-4-2, 33)

13.5 x 16 x 5.6 cm
Stela fragment, three lines of inscription remaining. Above is a band of chevrons.

1. [LRBT L] TNT PN B'L WL'DN
2. [L]B'L ḤMN 'Š NDR ḤMLK
3. BN ḤMLKT BN B'LḤN'

1) [To the lady] to Tanit face of Baal and to the lord 2) [to] Baal Hammon which vowed Himilk 3) son of Himilkot son of
Baalhanno.

BMPI pl. 23, 65; Euting 1883, 504; CIS I,2, 504

Pu70.125256 (57-12-18, 6)

29 x 13 x 8.5 cm
Stela, top missing but traces of two rows of incised egg and dart moulding and vertical lines remain. Roughened surface. Four-line inscription:

1. LRBT LTNT PN B
2. 'L WL'DN LB'L Ḥ
3. MN 'Š NDR' 'M'Š
4. TRT BT 'BRGH

1) To the lady to Tanit face of B 2)aal and to the lord to Baal Ha 3) mmon which vowed Am'ash 4) tart daughter of 'BRGH

BMPI pl. 3, 8; Euting 1883, 26; CIS I,2, 452

Pu71.125324 (57-12-18, 37)

41.3 x diam. 13.3 cm
Part of a column having inset niches with rounded arches arranged in three tiers. Roughened surface. Five-line

inscription:

1. LRBT LTNT PN B'L
2. WL'DN LB'L ḤMN 'Š
3. NDR BDMLQRT BN 'BD
4. MLQRT BN ḤMLKT KŠM
5. ' QL' YBRK'

1) To the lady to Tanit face of Baal 2) and to the lord to Baal Hammon which 3) vowed Bodmelqart son of 'Abd 4) melqart son of Himilkot for he hea 5) rd his voice, may he bless him.

Though its shape is unusual the inscription is the standard dedicatory type. It has been suggested that the column is a model watch tower or lighthouse (Harden) or a columbarium (Barnett pers. comm.).[34]

BMPI, pl. 26, 73; CIS I,1, 181; Cooke 1903, no. 48; Harden 1962, 1980, pl. 24, pp. 132, 304

Pu72. 125217 (59-4-2, 35)

3.0 x 15.7 x 19.4 cm

Marble plinth with a dedicatory inscription on two edges, probably a statue base.

1. [N]DR B'LŠLK [35]*BN 'KBR 'L BNM TŠM' QL'*
or possibly: *...BN MT ŠM' QL'*
2. TBRK'

1) Vow of Baalshillek son of 'Akbor for his son. May you hear his voice 2) and bless him' or alternatively, ' ...vow of... for his dead son. Hear his voice...

BMPI, pl. 25, 71; CIS I,1, 178; Lidzbarski 1898, 430. 6

There are a number of possible meanings of this inscription. It could be interpreted as evidence of a child sacrifice, a monument to a beloved son, or a vow for the health of a sick child. The temple of Eshmun at Sidon has produced a number of statues of children, one of which has a long one-line inscription on its plinth.[36] The statues were dedicated to Eshmun, the god of healing.

Pu73. 125281 (76-2-25, 5)

16.4 x 13.5 x 5.5 cm

Small fragment with part of two lines of inscription inset in an architectural frame.

1. ...HMQDŠM
2. ...'ŠMNḤLṢ BN

1)...the sanctuary/ sanctuaries... 2) Eshmunhilles son of ...

The meaning of these fragmentary lines is unclear. It has been suggested that it is part of an offering list and that Eshmunhilles was a suffete. However, this is unlikely – the inscription, even taking into account what is missing, is much too small. The most likely explanation is that this is a dedication plaque, set into the wall of a sanctuary or temple by the person who caused it to be built, i.e. Eshmunhilles. The inscription is short, only two lines and a very short third line, now missing, which probably gave the patronym. In the missing letters of the other two lines there is only room for five or six letters in the first line and three letters in the second.

From the Fenner Collection, 2
Euting 1871, pl. 12, 196 and p. 17; CIS I,1, 168

Pu74. 125303 (60-10-2, 18)

28 x 22.5 x 4.9 cm

Part of an inscribed plaque listing the payments for sacrifices and which portions go to the priests and which to the offerer. If the interpretation of the last remaining line is correct, it comes from a temple and was probably placed on a wall, so that those giving offering should know the rules. Eleven incomplete lines remain. The letters are well carved and the words are separated and do not run from one line to the next.

There are four other extant tariff texts, of which the most complete is the Marseilles tariff.[37]

1. B'T HMŠ'TT 'Š TN'...
2. ...RT LKHNM WTBRT LB'L HZBḤ
3. ...'RT LKHNM WTBRT LB'L HZBḤ
4. ...ṢW'T WKN 'RT H'ZM LKHNM WKN H'Š[L]...
5. ...ṢRB 'YL KLLM 'M ṢW'T WKN H'RT LKH[NM]...
6. ...Ḥ DL MQN' BL YKN LKHN MNM
7. ...BṢṢ KSP ZR // 'L 'ḤD
8. ...Š Y'MS BNT 'LM KN LKHN QṢRT W
9. ...QDŠT W'L ZBḤ ṢD W'L ZBḤ ŠMN...
10. ...'L ḤLB W'L ZBḤ BMNḤT W'L...
11. ...'YBL ŠT BPS Z WNḤ

1) Tariff of payment put up by... 2)... to the priests but the remainder shall belong to the person offering the sacrifice 3) ... skin to the priests but the remainder shall belong to the person offering the sacrifice 4) ... prayer-offering the skin of the goats shall go to the priests but the ?innards shall go... 5) ... the ?burnt offering of a hart, whole offerings, ?prayer offerings, the skin to the priests... 6) ... who is poor in cattle nothing of them shall go to the priest 7) ... for a ?blossom/wild one two silver zar(s) for each 8) ... [w]hich is carried before the gods there goes to the priest ?joints/portions and ... 9) ... sacred...and for a sacrifice of ?game and for a sacrifice of oil... 10) ... for milk and for a sacrifice of meal-offering and for... 11) ... [every payment which] is not set down on this board shall be give[n]...

Davis 1861, opp. p. 279; BMPI, pl. 32, 90; Cooke 1903, no. 43; CIS I,1, 167; Harden 1962, pl. 25, p. 120; KAI 74

Pu75. 125263 (76-2-25, 8)

9.5 x 35 x 11.8 cm

Fragment, possibly an altar step,[38] with a well- carved two-line inscription:

1. ḤDŠ WP'L 'YT HMṬBH[39]*Z DL P'MM*[40]*'ŠRT H'ŠM 'Š 'L HMQDŠM 'Š KN BŠT Š[PṬM]*

2. GRSKN WGR'ŠTRT BN YḤNB'L BN 'ZRB'L BN ŠPṬ WBD'ŠTRT BN...

1) The Decemvirs in charge of the sanctuaries renovated and made this sacrificial altar(literally, slaughtering table with legs/steps) which was in the year of the s[uffetes]

2) Gersakon and Ger'ashtart son of Yahonbaal son of 'Azrubaal son of Shafot and Bod'ashtart son...

Euting 1883, pl. 12.195; Lidzbarski 1898, 430.4; Cooke 1903, 130.46; CIS I,1, 175; KAI, vol. I, 98, no. 80

Pu76.125309 (59-4-2, 6)

33.6 x 11 x 10 cm

Gabled stela with four lines of inscription remaining:

1. LRBT LTNT PN B
2. 'L WL'DN LB'L Ḥ
3. MN 'Š NDR 'RŠ
4. M BN 'BDMLQR[T]

1) To the lady to Tanit face of B 2) aal and to the lord to Baal Ha 3)mmon which vowed Arish 4) am son of 'Abdmelqar[t].

BMPI, pl. 11, 31; Euting 1883, 49; CIS I,2, 473

Pu77.125297 (57-12-18, 15)

20 x 13 x 7.6 cm

Stela fragment, five lines of inscription remaining:

1. B'L Ḥ[MN] 'Š ND
2. R' 'RŠT BT
3. 'BDMLQRT
4. BN BD'ŠTRT
5. BN B'L'ZR

... 1) Baal Hammon which vow 2) ed Arishat daughter of 3) 'Abdmelqart 4) son of Bod'ashtart 5) son of Baal'azor.

BMPI, pl. 5, 15; Euting 1883, 33; CIS I,2, 459

Pu78.125302 (59-4-2, 28)

29 x 14.5 x 10.7 cm

Stela fragment, roughened surface, four lines of inscription remaining:

1. [WL]' DN LB'L Ḥ[MN]
2. 'Š NDR ḤMLKT BN
3. BD'ŠTRT BN ḤML
4. KT BN MHRB'L

1) and to the lord to Baal Ha[mmon] 2) which vowed Himilkot son of 3) Bod'ashtart son of Himil 4) kot son of Maharbaal.

BMPI, pl. 20, 57; Euting 1883, 75; CIS I,2, 496

Pu79.125259 (59-4-2, 1)

26 x 13.5 x 8.9 cm

Gabled stela. Roughened surface. Five-line inscription only:

1. LRBT LTNT PN B'L
2. WL'DN LB'L ḤMN
3. 'Š NDR ḤN' BN
4. ḤNB'L BN B'LML
5. 'K BN ḤMLKT BN

1) To the lady to Tanit face of Baal 2) and to the lord to Baal Hammon 3) which vowed Hanno son of 4) Hannibaal son of Baalmal 5) ok son of Himilkot son of...

BMPI pl. 4, 11; Euting 1883, 29; CIS I,2, 455

Pu80.125298 (60-10-2, 5)

16 x (at front) 8 x 8.5 cm

Stela, originally gabled, probably with acroteria. Traces of a symbol, possibly an arm and hand, in the pediment. An inscription of seven short lines is crudely scratched in the stone with the top of a letter ppossibly an 'l' on the 8th line.

1. LRBT[LT]
2. NT PN B
3. 'L WL'
4. DN LB'L
5. ḤMN 'Š N
6. DR ḤN'
7. B[N] 'KBR
8. ...[?L]

1) To the lady [to Ta] 2) nit face of B 3) aal and to the lo 4) rd to Baal Hammon which vo 6) wed Hanno 7) son of 'Akbor 8) ...[?L].

BMPI, pl. 28, 77; Euting 1883, 95; CIS I,2, 513

Pu81.125330 (59-4-2, 22)

13.1 x 12.6 x 5.6 cm

Stela fragment, roughened surface. Remains of two lines of inscription:

1. ḤN' BN BD[MLQR]
2. T BN ḤN' BN MG[N]

... 1) Hanno son of Bod[melqar] 2) t son of Hanno son of Mag[on].

BMPI, pl. 24, 69; Euting 1883, 87; CIS I,2, 507

Pu82.125278 (60-10-2, 13)

20 x 10.5 x 7 cm

Badly damaged and fragmented stela with gabled top. There appears to be a rudimentary human head in the apex, in profile to the left. Remains of a three-line inscription:

1. RBT LTNT [PN B'L
2. WL']DN LB'L Ḥ[MN]
3. ...[?']BD'[ŠMN]

1) [To the] lady to Tanit [face of Baal and 2) to] the lord to Baal Ha[mmon which vow 3) ed [?'A]bdEsh[mun]/ BodEsh[mun]...

BMPI pl. 30, 85; Euting 1883, 103; CIS I,2, 520

Pu83.125086 (59-4-2, 4; formerly S.O.C. 97)

24 x 10.5 x 10.6 cm

Gabled stela with five lines of inscription remaining. The inscription is crudely carved with misspellings and omissions:

1. LRB<T>[41] LTNT PN
2. B'L WL'DN N[42]
3. B'L ḤMN 'Š

4. NDR BDMLQR
5. T BN B'LḤN' B[N]

1) To the lady to Tanit face of 2) Baal and to the lord to 3) Baal Hammon which 4) vowed Bodmelqar 5) t son of Baalhanno s[on]...

BMPI pl. 11, 33; Euting 1883, 51; CIS I,2, 475

Pu84. 125246 (57-12-18, 31)

21 x 11 x 8 cm

Stela fragment, five lines of inscription remaining in addition to some bottom strokes from an upper line:

1. ... [ND]
2. R BDMLQR
3. T BN GRSKN
4. BN MLKYTN
5. KŠM' QL'
6. BR<K>'[43]

... 1) [vow] 2) ed Bodmelqar 3) t son of Gersakon 4) son of Milkyaton 5) for he heard his voice 6) (and) blessed him.

BMPI pl. 17, 49; Euting 1883, 67; CIS I,2, 488

Pu85. 125212 (57-12-18, 16)

16 x 7.5 cm

Stela fragment with the remains of six lines of inscription:

1. ...W[B']
2. LḤMN['Š]
3. NDR BDMLQ
4. RT BN ḤLṢ
5. B'L BN BDM
6. LQRT

1) ... and [Baa] 2) l Hammon [which] 3) vowed Bodmelq 4) art son of Hilllis 5) baal son of Bodme 6) lqart.

BMPI, pl. 6, 18; Euting 1883, 36; CIS I,2, 461

Pu86. 125240 (57-12-18, 51)

21 x 5.5-7.5 x 9 cm

Stela, broken lengthways so that only the first part of five lines of inscription remain:

1. LRBT L...
2. WL'DN...
3. 'Š [NDR]
4. BDMLQR[T BN 'D]
5. NB'L B[N]...

1) To the lady to... 2) and to the lord... 3) which [vowed] 4) Bodmelqar[t son of [?Ado] 5) nibaal s[on]....

BMPI pl. 16, 48; Euting 1883, 66; CIS I,2, 487

Pu87. 125242 (57-12-18, 18)

26.5 x 14 x 6 cm

Gabled stela. Rough surface. Five lines of inscription remain:

1. LRBT LTNT PN B
2. 'L WL'DN LB[']
3. L ḤMN 'Š NDR
4. BD'ŠTRT B[N]
5. 'BNB'L[44] *BN GR*

1) To the lady to Tanit face of B 2) aal and to the lord to B[aa] 3) l Hammon which vowed 4) Bod'ashtart son of 5) Abnbaal (or Adonibaal) son of Ger...

BMPI pl. 12, 35; Euting 1883, 53; CIS I,2, 476

Pu88. 125214 (57-12-18, 28

12.7 x 10 x 9.5 cm

Stela fragment, four lines of inscription:

1. ḤMN NDR BD
2. 'ŠTRT BN '
3. DNB'L BN B'
4. LŠPT BŠRM[45]

...1) Hammon, vow (of) Bod 2) 'ashtart son of A 3) donibaal son of Baa 4) lshafot BŠRM.

BMPI, pl. 6, 16; CIS I,1, 297
Cf. Bertrandy-Sznycer 1987, nos. 25, 104

Pu89. 125213 (60-10-2, 15)

12.5 x 17.5 x 7.5 cm

Stela fragment. Roughened surface. Three lines of inscription remain and the lower strokes of an upper line.

1. [L]R[BT LTNT PN B'L]
2. WL'DN LB'L ḤMN '
3. Š NDR BD'ŠTRT
4. BN ḤNB'L

1) [To the] l[ady to Tanit face of Baal] 2) and to the lord to Baal Hammon wh 3) ich vowed Bod'ashtart 4) son of Hannibaal.

BMPI, pl. 31, 87; Euting 1883, 105; CIS I,2, 522

Pu90. 125283 (57-12-18, 11)

19.5 x 11 x 6.5 cm

Stela with four lines of inscription remaining, most of the first line missing:

1. MN 'Š [NDR B]
2. 'L ḤN' BN B'LŠL
3. K BN BDMLQRT BN
4. MLQRTḤLṢ

...1) Hammon which [vowed B] 2) aalhanno son of Baalshille 3) k son of Bodmelqart son of 4) Melqarthilles.

BMPI pl. 10, 30; Euting 1883, 48; CIS I,2, 472

Pu91. 125268 (60-10-2, 12)

14 x 9 x 5.2 cm

Stela fragment with part of four lines of inscription remaining:

1. ...R B
2. 'LḤLṢ
3. BN BDM
4. LQRT

1) ...[vow]ed B 2) aalhilles 3) son of Bodme 4) lqart.

BMPI pl. 30, 86; Euting 1883, 104; CIS I,2, 521

Pu92. 125236 (59-4-2, 31)

18 x 14-15 x 9 cm

Stela fragment. Surface roughened. Four lines of inscription remaining:

1. ʻL ḤMN ʼŠ [N]
2. DR BʻLYT[N]
3. BN ZBG B[N]
4. ʻBDMLQR[T]

...[B] 1) aal Hammon which [vo] 2) wed Baalyat[on] 3) son of ZBG son of 4) ʻAbdmelqart.

BMPI pl. 21, 60; Euting 1883, 78; CIS I,2, 499 which sees another line above l. 1 which is not in BMPI or on the stone

Pu93. 125218 (76-2-25, 4)

15.2 x 9 x 4.5 cm

Stela fragment with five lines of inscription remaining. The inscription is badly carved and some letters can be read in different ways, giving rise to different interpretations of both the name of the dedicator and his patronymic.

1. LRBT LTNT PN
2. LʼDN LBʻL ḤMN [ʼŠ NDR]
3. Bʻ[46]LʻLK[47] BN K/NML[48]
4. [Y]BRK

1) To the lady to Tanit fa[ce of Baal] and 2) to the lord to Baal Hammon [which vowed] 3) BʻLʻLK son of K/NML 4) [May he] bless him.

From the Fenner Collection, 5
Euting 1871, p. 18 and pls. 13, 199; Euting 1883, 199; CIS I,2, 540

Pu94. 125288 (57-12-18, 19)

19 x 9 x 9.6 cm

Gabled stela. Roughened surface. Five lines of inscription remain:

1. LRBT LTNT[49]
2. PN BʻL WLʼDN
3. LBʻL ḤMN
4. ʼŠ NDR[ʼ B][50]
5. TBʻL BT

1) To the lady to Tanit 2) face of Baal and to the lord 3) to Baal Hammon 4) which vowed [B] 5) tbaal daughter of ...

BMPI pl. 9, 27; Euting 1883, 45; CIS I,2, 469

Pu95. 125262 (57-12-18, 36)

8 x 12 x 10.7 cm

Stela fragment, inscription only, scratched crudely on the stone:

1. ...GDNʻM
2. BT ʼRŠT NDR
3. MGN BN ḤNʼ[51]

1)...Gadnaam 2) daughter of Arishat the vow of 3) Magon son of Hanno.

BMPI pl. 14, 42; Euting 1883, 60; CIS I,1, 383

Pu96. 125255 (59-4-2, 2)

29 x 14 x 10.5 cm

Gabled stela, four lines of inscription remaining:

1. [L]RBT LTN[T]
2. PN BʻL WLʼD
3. N LBʻL ḤMN ʼ[Š]
4. NDR ZYWG BN

1) [To] the lady to Tani[t] 2) face of Baal and to the lo 3) rd to Baal Hammon which 4) vowed Zivag son of....

BMPI pl. 6, 17; Euting 1883, 35; CIS I,2, 460

Pu97. 125314 (57-12-18, 21)

26 x 9.4 x 9 cm

Stela fragment. Roughened surface, six lines of inscription:

1. LRBT LTNT
2. PN BʻL WLʼ
3. DN LBʻL ḤM
4. N ʼŠ NDRʼ K
5. BDT BT ʻZ
6. R BN ʻBDʼ

1) To the lady to Tanit 2) face of Baal and to the lo 3) rd to Baal Hammo 4) n which vowed Ka 5) bdot daughter of ʻAz 6) or son of Abdo.

BMPI, pl. 3,9; Euting 1883, 27; CIS I,2, 453

Pu98. 125312 (59-4-2, 3)

32.6 x 14.5 x 10.4 cm

Gabled stela, roughened surface, five lines of inscription remaining:

1. LRBT LTNT
2. PN BʻL WLʼ
3. DN[52] LBʻL Ḥ
4. MN ʼŠ NDR
5. MHRB[ʻL BN]...

1) To the lady to Tanit 2) face of Baal and to the lo 3) rd to Baal Ha 4) mmon which vowed 5) Mahar[baal] son of...

BMPI, pl. 11, 32; Euting 1883, 50; CIS I,2, 474

Pu99. 125306 (59-4-2, 15)

21 x 18 x 9.5 cm

Gabled stela with acroteria. The roughened surface makes it difficult to read the inscription. Poorly written three-line inscription:

1. LRBT TNT PN BʻL WLDN[53]
2. LBʻL ḤMN ʼŠ NDR MTN
3. BʻL BT GR[SK]N BN BʻL
4. ...[L]T[54]

1) To the lady Tanit face of Baal and to the lord 2) to Baal Hammon which vowed Muttun 3) baal daughter of Ger[sak]on son of Baal 4)... *[L]T*

BMPI, pl. 19, 56; Euting 1883, 74; CIS I,2, 495

Pu100.125231 (59-4-2, 26)

17.8 x 11 x 4 cm

Stela fragment. Two lines of inscription remain plus the bottom strokes of an upper line perhaps ḤMN 'Š NDR:

1. MTNB'L BT
2. YTNB'L

...1) Muttunbaal daughter of 2) Yatonbaal.

BMPI pl. 22,63; Euting 1883, 81; CIS I,2, 502

Pu101.125220 (59-4-2, 32)

16 x 13.3 x 10 cm

Badly worn stela fragment. Only the bottom line is legible but fragments of two other lines are visible. One line has been partly read in BMPI and CIS (the stone surface has deteriorated since then):

1. ...[?]...
2. ML[KYTN]BN MH[R]B'L BN
3. MLKYTN TŠM' QL'

1)... 2) Mil[kyaton] son of Mah[ar]baal son of 3) Milkyaton may you/she hear his voice.

BMPI, pl. 24, 68; Euting 1883, 86; CIS I,2, 506

Pu102.125296 (57-12-18, 22)

25 x 11 x 8 cm

Gabled stela with roughened surface. Four-line inscription:

1. LRBT LTNT PN
2. B'L WL'DN LB
3. 'L ḤMN 'Š ND
4. R NBG BN PRŠ [55]

1) To the lady to Tanit 2) face of Baal and to the lord to B 3) aal Hammon which vo 4) wed Nabag son of Parosh.

BMPI, pl. 3, 7; Euting 1883, 25; CIS I,2, 451

Pu103.125290 (59-4-2, 21)

18 x 12 x 7.6 cm

Battered stela fragment with five lines of inscription remaining:

1. [B]'L WL'D[N LB'L]
2. [Ḥ]MN 'Š NDR 'B
3. D'ŠMN HSPR
4. BN 'BDMLQR
5. T

1) [B]aal and to the lor[d to Baal 2) Ha]mon which vowed 'Ab 3) deshmun the scribe 4) son of 'Abdmelqar 5) t.

BMPI pl. 15,43; Euting 1883, 61; CIS I,1, 241

Pu104.125301 (59-4-2, 11)

26.5 x 14.9 x 8.5 cm

Gabled stela with acroteria. Complete four-line inscription clearly but inelegantly carved. The letters of lines 2 and 3 were not spaced properly and the mason had to squeeze the last letters of the lines almost on to the edge of the face. Also, some letters are more lightly cut than others.

1. LRBT LTNT PN B'L
2. WL'DN LB'L ḤMN '
3. Š NDR 'BD'ŠMN B
4. N 'BDTNT

1) To the lady to Tanit face of Baal 2) and to the lord to Baal Hammon wh 3) ich vowed 'Abdeshmun so 4) n of 'Abdtanit.

BMPI, pl. 22, 62; Euting 1883, 80; CIS I,2, 501

Pu105.125273 (60-10-2, 8)

11 x 13 x 8.9 cm

Stela fragment, four-line inscription remaining:

1. LRBT LTNT PN B'L
2. WL'DN LB'L ḤMN
3. 'Š NŠ' 'BD'ŠMN
4. BN ṢLḤ TŠM' [56] *QL[']*

1) To the lady to Tanit face of Baal 2) and to the lord to Baal Hammon 3) which offered 'Abdeshmun 4) son of Selah, may you/she hear his voice.

BMPI, pl. 29, 83; Euting 1883, 101; CIS I,1, 411

Pu106.125257 (59-4-2, 17)

28 x 16.5 x ? cm

Stela fragment, four lines of inscription and one letter of an upper line remain:

1. ...N...
2. [Š]NDR 'BD'[ŠMN B]
3. N BD'ŠTRT BN[B]
4. 'LḤN' BN BD'ŠT
5. RT

1) ...N... 2) ...vowed 'Abde[shmun so] 3) n of Bo[d'a]shtart son of [B] 4) aalhanno son of Bod'ashta 5) rt.

BMPI pl. 21, 59 which see 'L' on l. 1; Euting 1883, 77; CIS I,2, 498

Pu107.125235 (59-4-2, 8)

23 x 13 x 9 cm

Stela fragment with gabled top. Surface roughened. Five lines of inscription remaining:

1. LRBT LTNT
2. PN B'L WL'D
3. N LB'L ḤMN
4. 'Š NDR 'BD
5. 'ŠMN BN...

1) To the lady to Tanit 2) face of Baal and to the lo 3) rd to Baal Hammon which vowed 'Abd 5) eshmun son of...

BMPI pl. 5, 14; Euting 1883, 32; CIS I,2, 458

Pu108.125229 (59-4-2, 18)

16.5 x 10 x 9 cm

Stela, top missing, roughened surface. Five lines of inscription only remaining:

1. *...R 'BDML*
2. *QRT BN 'ZR*
3. *B'L BN ḤM*
4. *L<Q>RT BN B'L*
5. *ŠLK*

1)...[which vow]ed 'Abdmel 2) qart son of 'Azru 3) baal son of Himi 4) l<q>art son of Baal 5) shillek.

BMPI, pl. 17, 51; Euting 1883, 69; CIS I,2, 490 which reads BDMLQRT on l.1-2 and ḤMLKT on l. 3-4

Pu109.125241 (59-4-2, 29)

25 x 14 x 7 cm

Stela fragment, remains of four lines of inscription:

1. *DR['BD]...*
2. *'BDMLQRT BN '*
3. *BD'ŠMN BN GRS*
4. *KN*

1) [v]owed ['BD] 2) 'Abdmelqart son of 'A 3) bdeshmun son of Gersa 4) kon.

BMPI pl. 22, 61; Euting 1883, 79; CIS I,2, 500 which restores l. 1 completely though the stone is broken after the possible 'D'

Pu110. 125313 (59-4-2, 5)

34 x 13.4 x 7 cm

Gabled stela with five lines of inscription remaining:

1. *[LRBT LT]NT PN*
2. *[B]'L WL'DN LB'*
3. *[L] ḤMN 'Š NŠ'*
4. *['BD* or *BD]MLQRT BN Ṣ/Z*
5. *...BN 'ZML[K]*

1) To the lady to Tanit face of 2) [B]aal and to the lord to Baa 3) [l] Hammon which offered ['Abd or Bod]melqart son of Ṣ/Z 5) ...son of 'Azimil[k].

BMPI, pl. 8, 23 restores 'ABD; Euting 1883, 41; CIS I,1, 412 restores BD

Pu111.125243 (59-4-2, 19)

25 x 11 x 8 cm

Stela fragment, six broken lines of inscription remaining:

1. *LRBT...*
2. *PN B'L WL['DN]*
3. *LB'L ḤMN '[Š N]*
4. *DR 'ZRB'L[B]*
5. *N MHRB'L[B]*
6. *N ḤNB'L*

1) To the lady... 2) face of Baal and to the Lo[rd]... 3) to Baal Hammon wh[ich vo] 4) wed 'Azrubaal [s] 5) on of Maharbaal [s] 6) on of Hannibaal.

BMPI pl. 12, 36; Euting 1883, 54; CIS I,2, 477

Pu112.125215 (57-12-18, 32)

11 x 11 x 9.5 cm

Stela fragment, roughened surface, three lines of inscription remaining:

1. *WL'DN LB'L ḤMN*
2. *'Š NDR 'LŠT B[T]*
3. *B'L'ZR BN KN*[57]*...*

1) and to the lord to Baal Hammon 2) which vowed 'Alshat [daughter of] 3) Baal'azor son of KN....

BMPI pl. 14, 40; Euting 1883, 58; CIS I,2, 481

Pu113.125270 (57-12-18, 34)

15.5 x 10 x 7.9 cm

Gabled stela fragment, with acroteria. Two short lines of inscription remain, and the top of a *lamed* on a third line, below a plain carved lintel:

1. *LRBT L*
2. *TNT PN B[']*
3. *[W'DN]L...*

1) To the lady to 2) Tanit face of B[aa] 3) l...[and to the Lord] to...

BMPI pl. 18, 54; Euting 1883, 72; CIS I,2, 493

Pu114.125274 (60-10-2, 9)

10 x 11.5 x 9.1 cm

Stela fragment with two lines of inscription remaining :

1. *LRBT LTNT*
2. *PN'*[58] *B'L WL...*

1) To the lady to Tanit 2) face of Baal and to...

BMPI, pl. 29, 82; Euting 1883, 100; CIS I,2, 518

Pu115.125310 (59-4-2, 30)

34 x 10.5-13 x 6.9 cm

Damaged stela with eight lines of inscription, the top line mostly illegible:

1. *[LRBT LTNT PN]*
2. *[B'L]WL'DN LB*
3. *['L ḤM]N 'Š NDR*
4. *...BN GR'Š*
5. *[TRT]HṬBḤ*
6. *[BN]'DNB'L BN '*
7. *[ZR]B'L HRB TŠM*[59]
8. *[' QL']*

1) [To the lady to Tanit face] 2) [of Baal] and to the lord to B 3) [aal Hamm]on which vowed 4) ...son of Ger'ash 5) [tart] the slaughterer[60]... 6) [son of] Adonibaal son of 'A 7) [zrub]aal the chief, may you/she hear 8) his voice.

BMPI pl. 23, 66; Euting 1883, 84; CIS I,1, 237

Pu116.125275 (60-10-2, 10)

13 x 7-10 x 12.7 cm

Stela fragment with the remains of five lines of inscription:

1. ...NT PN B'...
2. L ḤMN 'Š N...
3. BT B'LḤN'...
4. BN BD'ŠTRT
5. ... L...

1) [To the lady to Ta]nit face of Baa 2) [l and to the lord to Baa] 3) l Hammon which vo[wed...]/ daughter of Baalhanno... 4) son of Bod'ashtart.

BMPI, pl. 29, 81; Euting 1883, 99; CIS I,2, 517

Pu117.125294 (59-4-2, 20)

23 x 13.5 x 7.4 cm

Stela fragment with three lines of inscription remaining, the top line almost gone:

1. ...RT BN
2. ḤMLKT KŠM
3. ' QL' TBRK'

1)...rt son of 2)Himilkot for hear 3)ing his voice may you bless him.

BMPI, pl. 24, 70; Euting 1883, 88; CIS I,2, 508

Notes

1 Tombstones are not part of Punic culture until well into the Roman period.
2 It is possible that these three objects came from a temple or place of sacrifice connected to the Carthage tophet.
3 Though found at Marseilles the inscription may have come from a temple at Carthage. See *CIS* I, 165, Cooke 1903, no. 42, p. 112-122.
4 Segert 1976, p 274
5 Sader 1991, 121, figs. 4 and 20.
6 Note the *aleph* (') rather than the more common and etymologically correct *ayin* (').
7 The stroke in the centre of the *m* in Magon has been omitted.
8 *P'N* instead of *PN*, more common in the neo-Punic period.
9 There is a space for another letter, perhaps an '.
10 The inscription ends here though there is space for the father's name.
11 See Brown 1991,p. 126-7, where she provides a synopsis of the different theories.
12 *BN* was originally omitted and, as no space was left for it, the letters when inserted were carved very small and almost vertically from bottom to top.
13 Both CIS and Euting have read the name as 'Yakonshalim' but the *zayin* seems clear. It may be an error by the mason for an intended *yod*. On the other hand, ZKN has been read, doubtfully, in CIS 5610. In the later periods Y is sometimes written as a Z.
14 This is a mason's error and should be a *nun*, i.e. 'son'.
15 The mason carved a *daled* instead of a *resh*.
16 BMPI reads the name as 'RM, CIS as an error for 'Abdmilk. The most likely explanation is that the mason accidentally omitted the *B*.
17 *Cf.* Hours Miédan, pl. X.c (CIS 618) where there is a Tanit symbol in the palm.
18 The *taw* in *RBT* has been omitted.
19 BMPI has read the name, doubtfully, as 'Aberrath.
20 The space allocated for the inscription was filled when this letter was reached; this is probably a truncated form of Bodmelqart.
21 Vocalisation uncertain
22 A close inspection of the stela revealed that the first letter of the name, though faint, is a *yod*. The name is not unknown: *Cf.* Benz 1972, 329.
23 Instead of the more usual 'AMTB'L
24 *Aleph* instead of the more correct orthography with *ayin*.
25 The inscription finishes here.
26 'DN with an *ayin* instead of *aleph*.
27 The *m* lacks the short vertical stroke in the middle.
28 Note the unusual shape of the 'Z'.
29 Euting read this as the top line, but it is now illegible.
30 Euting 1883, pl. 198, 360 (see **Fig. 5)** shows a Tanit symbol with a *taw* in the triangle. Brown 1991, fig. 35, 522, illustrates a combined standard/caduceus with a *beth* and a *taw* on either side.
31 *Aleph* instead of *ayin*.
32 CIS reads ' Hanno son of...' (*Ḥ [N' BN]*
33 CIS suggests ' Maharbaal'.
34 A stela fragment showing part of a similar column with niches on a stepped base is illustrated in Brown 1991, fig. 38. She also states that there are five monuments in the Carthage Museum of column shape though she does not say whether they have niches.
35 BMPI reads *B'LMLK*.
36 See J. Gibson, *Textbook of Syrian Semitic Inscriptions, Vol. III*, (1982) no. 29; Doumet-Serhal, *et al*, *Stones and Creed* (Beirut 1997), no. 28.
37 *CIS* I, 165, Cooke 1903, no. 42. The others are *CIS* I, 170, *CIS* I,3915 and CIS I,3917
38 The size, especially the depth, of the fragment suggests this.
39 Previously read as ' slaughterhouse' but perhaps a place of ritual sacrifice or a sacrificial altar. Hoftizer-Jongeling calls it a slaughtering table *MTBH*
40 ?Steps or base.
41 *taw* omitted.
42 *nun* instead of *lamed*.
43 The *kaf* has been omitted but there is a space for it.
44 Corrected by CIS to *'DNB'L*.
45 The meaning of *BŠRM* is uncertain. Tomback 1978, 57-8, considers it a type of sacrifice, Cooke 1903, 138, a place-name, probably Cirta. Charlier 1953 discusses the meaning in ' Les stèles puniques de Constantine et la question des sacrifice dits "Molchomor" en relation avec l'expression *"BŠRMBTM"*. CIS I,1, 365 also contains a discussion of its meaning. See also Bertrandy-Sznycer 1987, 82 for a discussion of the problem.
46 The *ayin* is only half carved.
47 Probably a misspelling of Baalshillek but CIS gives the name as written.
48 *KML* is unknown though *NML* does appear (*cf.* CIS I,2, 635, 725, 894). Euting 1871 goes further and sees the possibility of *NTN* though his first reading is *KML*. Benz, 1972, 147, sees *NML*[*M*].
49 The *n* in Tanit has been so lightly carved that it is almost invisible, leading BMPI and CIS to conclude that it was omitted.
50 BMPI restores ' in l. 4 and suggests the name *Amotbaal* or *Batbaal*.
51 Magon son of Hanno seems out of place unless this is a dual dedication, perhaps by husband and wife.
52 Both Euting and CIS see the *daled* as a misspelled *beth* but it is properly written; the roughened surface has caused a deep scratch at the bottom of the *daled*.
53 The *lamed* before 'Tanit' and the *aleph* in *L'DN* have been omitted.
54 CIS reads a misspelled Baalshillek, BMPI restores *TT* on l. 4.
55 CIS and Euting read ' Nebo son of Arish' but both the *gimmel* and the *peh* are clear. *PR'Š* is known (Benz 1972, 395).
56 ' instead of '
57 CIS suggests *'Kanbaal'*.
58 The strange spelling foreshadows the breakdown of the orthography in neo-Punic. [MW]
59 The final letter has been omitted, probably because the mason misjudged the spacing and ran out of room.
60 Clearly an important religious office. The word has a number of other possible meanings, i.e., executioner, butcher, but this is the most likely.

Neo-Punic Stelae

NPu1. 125056 (S.O.C.4)

45.8 x 23 x ? cm

Stela with gabled top. Smoothed surface. In the inset pediment is a stylised bucranium. In a square inset niche below is a combined Tanit-baetyl symbol with upraised arms. The background of the inset areas has been chiselled away so as to create the symbols which are in a low flat relief. In the frame between pediment and niche is a two-line neo-Punic inscription usually with spacing between the words and with a larger space following the first word in line 2:

1. ND'R 'Š N'DR ḤN' BN MTNB'L
2. ŠYPŠ PG' 'ZRM H'Š

1) The vow which vowed Hanno son of Muttunbaal
2) ?tribute/?gift. He discharged this *AZRM* sacrifice.

The inscription resembles those from Guelma (Calama) in Algeria, discussed by Chabot, but the decoration is stylistically closer to stelae from el-Hofra (Constantine) where many of the Tanit symbols have similar upraised arms and are executed in flat relief. Bucrania are rare, although there is a bull's head on a stela from Carthage.[1] Here, the bucranium may be the symbol of a deity, probably Baal Hammon, not an indication of the type of sacrifice.

2nd-1st century BC
Gesenius, *Script. Ling. Phoen. Mon.* pl. 24; Schröder 1869, 65, 265.4 (NP 11); Chabot 1916c, 516 (= *Punica,* 90); H.P. Roschinski, in *Texte aus der Umwelt des Alten Testaments*, II/4 (1988), 619; Mendleson 1995, 260, fig. 8.
Cf. Hoftizer-Jongeling, DISI, 642-43, s.v. MLK5, sub 4

NPu2. 125117 (57-12-18, 44)

77.5 x 39 x ? cm

Gabled stela with decoration in low flat relief and a four-line neo-Punic inscription. In the pediment is a twelve-petalled rosette in a disk. Below it is a Tanit symbol made up of a disc in a crescent with raised ends for the head and arms and a triangle below this for the body. On either side of the figure is a raised disc. Below is another Tanit symbol with raised arms. It is flanked by ornate caducei with arrow-shaped shafts. Below the 'Tanit' is an inset square with raised border within which is the incised four-line votive inscription:

1. L'DN LB'L NDR 'Š NDR
2. G'Y Y'LY 'RŠ
3. BN 'DNB'L BN 'DRB'L
4. KH ŠM' QL' BRK'

1) To the lord to Baal a vow which vowed 2) Gaius Julius Arish 3) son of Adonibaal son of Addirbaal 4) for he heard his voice and he blessed him.

Very cursive writing: the same sign, a small vertical stroke, slightly slanted, is used without differentiation for *three* letters, *B, D, R*.

The style is similar to that of stelae from el-Hofra (Constantine) and other Numidian sites from the 2nd century BC on (*cf.* Berthier-Charlier 1952, pl. XXVIIa) with its raised, flat decoration in the Punic tradition. The dedicant's name is a mixture of Latin and Punic though the father and grandfather have Punic names.

Schröder 1869, 72 (NP 112); Chabot 1917b, 33, no. 3 (*Punica*, 144); M'charek 1988, 745; Mendleson 1995, 260 and fig. 9.
Cf. Bertrandy-Sznycer 1987, nos. 13, 38, for similar iconography but with a Punic inscription.

NPu3. 125100 (58-6-3, 2)

44.5 x 37.4 x 12 cm

Stela, top part missing. Three-line inscription in an inset rectangular panel with the letters hanging down from lightly scored lines. On either side is a thin rectangular inset panel. Above, with the background cut away, is a Tanit symbol with raised arms (head missing), probably within a niche (the side pieces are also in raised flat relief). Flanking this, also in inset panels, are two symbols with the top broken off, caducei or stylised trees, each having two sunken circles with raised centres on a double stalk.

Three-line votive neo-Punic inscription:

1. L'DN LB'L ND'R 'Š NDR ḤMLK
2. BN 'ZRB'L BN MTNB'L K'N K'N
3. ŠM' QL' <W>BR'K'

1) To the lord to Baal a vow which vowed Himilk 2) son of 'Azrubaal son of Muttunbaal for for [*sic*] 3) he heard his voice <and> blessed him.

Very cursive writing: the same small sign is used for two letters (*D, R*); the *nun* (*N*) and the *taw* (*T*) are not clearly distinguished. The scribe is quite inept, deforming the *beth* (*B*) in line three as well as the first *kaph* (*K*) in line two. Note the repetition of the preposition *K'N*, 'for, because', an expanded form of *K*, which is normally written in neo-Punic *K', K', KH* or *KḤ*

Presented by Sir Thomas Phillips, Bt., ex-Reade Collection
Bourgade 1852, 8, no. 6; Schröder 1869, 69 (*NP41*); Chabot 1917a, 150, no. 8 (*Punica*, 99).

NPu4. 125069 (57-12-18, 42)

39 x 34.5 x 7.5 cm

Bottom part of stela with three-line inscription in neo-Punic and Latin inset in a raised frame but itself raised from the background. Above is the triangle of a Tanit symbol flanked by standards with double shafts, on rectangular pedestals. The words of the inscription are separated.

1. L'DN LB'L NDR 'Š NDR
2. CRES
3. ŠM' QL' BRK'

1) To the lord to Baal a vow which vowed 2) CRES 3) he heard his voice, he blessed him.

Bourgade 1852, 6, no. 1; Schröder 1869, 68 (NPu35), 266.13, pl. XVI.11; Chabot 1917a, 147, no. 2 (*Punica*, 96); C.I.L. VIII, 1008

NPu5. 125195 (57-12-18, 49)

38 x 24 x ? cm

Stela fragment. Below, within a raised rectangular frame, is a six-line neo-Punic inscription. Above it is the bottom of a Tanit symbol in flat relief. On either side is the shaft of a standard or stylised tree also in flat relief. The shafts have raised flat circles along their length and splayed-out bases. The circles on the two shafts are not symmetrical.

1. *NDR LB'L*
2. *MṢQY QRT*
3. *LY KṢTY*
4. *'ŠM'*
5. *QL'*
6. *BRK'*

1) Vow to Baal 2) MSQY Qartu 3) llus Cestius[2] 4) hear his 5) voice 6) bless him.

Schröder 1869, 72 (NPu114); Chabot 1917b, 34, no. 5 (*Punica*, 145).

NPu6. 125105 (57-12-18, 47)

36 x 31.5 x ?cm

Stela fragment. Decoration in low flat relief. In the centre is a five-line inscription in a rectangular panel with raised border. Above this is the bottom of a Tanit symbol. On either side are parts of a standard or stylised tree with a high splayed-out base from which emerges a double shaft which curves outward and then in again to form circles with inset centres, the whole possibly derived from the caduceus symbol.

1. *L'DN LB'L ND'R 'Š N*
2. *'DR' B'L'NG B'*
3. *T ŠPṬ <BN> or <'ŠT> ḤNB'L BN 'B*
4. *DMLQRT K'N K'N BRK' Š*
5. *M' QL*

1) To the lord to Baal a vow which v 2) owed Baaloneg[3] daught 3) er of Shafot <son of> or <wife of> Hannibaal son of 'Ab 4) dmelqart that surely blessed her and hear 5) d <her> voice.

Schröder 1869, 72 (NPu111); Chabot 1917b, 32, no. 2 (*Punica* 143)
Cf. Bisi 1967, fig. 91 for an almost identical standard, provenance unknown and **Fig. 3** for a similar stela with leafy finial. NPu16 and 17, in similar style, also show leafy finials.

NPu7. 125196 (57-12-18, 46)

22.5 x 31.5 x 8.5 cm

Stela fragment with detail in flat relief. Within a rectangular panel with raised border is a three-line inscription. Above it is the bottom of a Tanit symbol flanked by the bottoms of standards/stylised trees on a wide rectangular plinth.

1. *L'DN LB'L ḤMN NDR ŠYPK*
2. *BT TZ'BŠ[4] ŠM'*
3. *QL' B[R]K'*

1) To the lord to Baal Hammon the vow of Shifak 2) daughter of Tizabesh, hear 3) her voice and bless her.

Chabot 1917b, 36, no. 9 (*Punica*, 147)

NPu8. 125050 (57-12-18, 43)

50.6 x 33.5 x 10.5 cm

Part of a stela with a three-line neo-Punic inscription inset in a rectangular frame with a double raised border. Above it is the triangle of a Tanit symbol. At the side is a standard with wide base, also in relief, topped by a circle with an inset centre, possibly part of a caduceus or stylized tree (see Bisi 1967, fig. 91, for the tree and Bertrandy-Sznycer 1987, 130, no. 79 for the caduceus).

1. *L'DN LB'L NDR*
2. *MS/ŠNGD'T[5] BN*
3. *'BDM[L]QRT*

1) To the lord to Baal a vow 2) of MS/ŠNGD'T (very tentative) son of 3) 'Abdme[l]qart.

The inscription is negligently written and the characters are haphazardly spaced so that the name of the dedicant is garbled.

Bourgade 1852, 7, no. 3; Schröder 1869, 68 (NPu37); Chabot 1917a, 148, no. 4 (*Punica*, 97)

NPu9. 125194 (57-12-18, 48)

42.5 x 23 x 7 cm

Stela, top part missing. Below, an incised five-line inscription in a square panel with raised border. Above, in flat relief is the bottom of a Tanit symbol with part of a standard/stylised tree on her right. It has a widened base and a circle with depressed centre on the shaft.

1. *L'DN LB'L ND*
2. *'R 'Š NDR' [B']L*
3. *'NG B'T B'NK Š[P]*
4. *Ṭ BRK...N*
5. *KḤN Š[M]' [Q]L' BRK'*

1) To the lord to Baal a vo 2) w which vowed [Baa]l 3) oneg daughter of Banok the suff 4) ete BRK....N 5) for he heard her voice; he blessed her.

Bourgade 1852, 6, no. 2; Schröder 1869, 68 (NPu36); Chabot 1917a, 147, no. 3 (*Punica*, 96).

NPu10. 125045 (57-12-18, 38)

49.6 x 30.5 x 13.1 cm

Part of stela with a four-line inscription inset in a square frame with a raised border. The decoration is both incised and relief. Above the inscription is a large twelve-petalled rosette within a double circle. Flanking it are standards or caducei on bases with concave sides. There is a faint trace of another symbol above the rosette, perhaps a crescent. The stela is efficiently and capably decorated in a precise geometrical manner.

1. *L'DN LB'L NDR 'Š NDR*
2. *Y'LṢS'N BN BRKB'L BN*
3. *BŠTS'N[6] KḤN KḤN[7] ŠM'*
4. *QL' BRK'*

1) To the lord to Baal a vow which vowed 2) Yaalsasan son of Barikbaal son of 3) BŠTS'N for he surely heard 4) his voice; he blessed him.

Bourgade 1852, 9, no. 7; Schröder 1869, 69 (NPu42), 267.15; Chabot 1917a, 150, no. 9 (*Punica*, 99).

NPu11.125057 (57-12-18, 45)

33 x 31 x 9 cm

Part of stela with a two-line neo-Punic inscription, probably funerary, within a lightly inset square frame with a slightly raised border. Above are parts of symbols in raised flat relief. In the centre is a pedestal flanked by L-shaped columns (see Bisi 1967, fig. 95, for a possible comparison). On the left is a circle raised on the outside with a depression in which is a raised boss.

Inscription:

1. Š 'DNB'L BN

2. 'BDMLQRT

1) Of (or: belonging to) Adonibaal son of 2) 'Abdmelqart.

The relative *Š* appears to indicate that this is a funerary inscription, as is the case on other inscriptions, for example on ossuaries. 'Tombstone' or 'belonging to' is therefore understood. However, one cannot entirely exclude the possibility of it being a votive stela, though this does appear to be less probable.

Bourgade 1852, 23, no. 38; Schröder 1869, 69 (NPu71); 1917a, 165, no. 37 (*Punica*, 114).

NPu12.125118 (59-4-2, 36)

32.5 x 34.5 x 10 cm

Part of a stela with a four-line inscription inset in a rectangular frame with raised border and 'swallow-tail' sides. Above is a Tanit symbol with raised arms (head missing) in flat relief. On either side a large circle is drilled deeply into the stone. The inscription is badly written and is full of errors.

1. L'DN B['[]LMN [8] *NDR*

2. M'ḤL' BN HBK

3. TY[Z]' KŠM' QL'

4. BRK'

1) To the lord Baal MN.(Baal Hammon) the vow of 2) Mehla son of HBK 3) TY[Z]' for he heard his voice; he 4) blessed him.

Chabot 1917b, 36-7, no. 10 (*Punica*, 147-8).

NPu13.125198 (59-4-2, 37)

32.5 x 29 x 8 cm

Part of stela, top missing. Decoration in flat relief with a short three-line (possibly funerary) inscription within a raised rectangular frame. Next to it is a standard/stylised tree: a double shaft on a wide base, the tops bending out at an angle just below the missing part of the stela.

1. Š 'ZR

2. B'L BN

3. YLGM

1) Of 'Azru 2) baal son of 3) YLGM.

Schröder 1869, 72 (NPu116); Chabot 1917b, 35, no. 7 (*Punica*, 146). *Cf.* NPu 11 and discussion of a similar type of inscription.

NPu14.125981 (57-12-18, 50)

27 x 20-16 x 8-9.5 cm

Bottom part of stela with the unfinished base which is normally set into the ground still in place. On one side, in a panel with raised border, are three lines of an inscription. Next to it and slightly above is the base of a standard or caduceus in flat relief.

1. L'DN LB...

2. MTNHYB'L BT M...

3. ŠM' QL' B[RK']

1) To the lord to B[aal]... 2) Mutunhibaal daughter of M... 3) he heard her voice; he b[lessed her].

Schröder 1869, 72 (NP 115); Chabot 1917b, 34-5, no. 6 (*Punica*, 145-6)

NPu15.125119 (59-4-2, 39)

29 x 35 x 12 cm

Stela fragment. A three-line inscription remains, inset in a rectangular raised frame with a double line above. The letters are deeply incised and very clear.

1. NDR(?)L B'L 'Š NDR QRNṬ'

2. BN BDB'L ŠM' QL'

3. BRK'

1)...to Baal which vowed Cornutus 2) son of Bodbaal hear his voice 3) he blessed him.

Bourgade 1852, 10, no. 11; Schröder 1869, 69 (NP 46); Chabot 1917a, 153, no. 13 (*Punica*, 102).

NPu16.125103 (58-6-3, 3)

35 x 36.5 x ? cm

Fragment of stela showing signs of decomposition. Above is a whimsical Tanit symbol consisting of a triangle within a raised frame topped by a flat circle. The figure's arms are leaves. On one side is the top of a large three-leaved standard/tree. Next to it is a rectangular panel with raised border with an illegible four- line inscription. Emanating from the panel is another large leaf.

Presented by Sir Thomas Phillips, Bt., ex-Reade Collection
Chabot 1917b, 38, no. 12 (*Punica*, 149).

NPu17.136681 (58-6-3, 4)

30 x 22 x 4 cm

Stela fragment in poor condition, parts flaking and repaired. The decoration is in low flat relief. Above is the base of a standard or caduceus. Below it, on one side, is what remains of a raised panel containing an inscription of ?five lines. Next to it is a three-leaved plant or standard on a hemispherical base.

1. L'DN L[B'L]

2. NDR 'Š [NDR]

3. 'BDMLQR[T BN]

4. MTN KḤ Š[M'..

5. QL' BR[K']

1) To the Lord to [Baal] 2) the vow which [vowed] 3)'Abedmelqar[t son of] 4) Muttun for hear[ing] his

5) voice (and) blessing [him].

Chabot noted that the first two lines of the inscription, which contain the dedicatory formula, are much larger than the rest and suggested that they were written earlier. This accords with what was general practice with stelae 'mass' produced in workshops and individual touches such as names being added later. This fragment and NPu 16 are so similar that they must have come from the same site and been made in the same workshop. Not only are the designs alike, particularly in the three-leaved finial, but they both show a similar pattern of decomposition.

Presented by Sir Thomas Phillips, Bt., ex-Reade Collection
Chabot 1917b, 37, no. 11 (*Punica*, 148-9).
Cf. **Fig. 3** after Bourgade 1852, no. 9, for an almost complete stela of the same type.

NPu18. 125090 (58-6-3, 1)

61 x 39 x 12 cm

Stela, top broken off, containing a large, almost square panel with raised border. In the panel is an incised four-line inscription with the letters written hanging down from ruled lines; the letters in the last line have been squeezed together in order to complete the inscription within the available space. Above the inscription is a scene depicting two winged figures on either side of a large bird (dove?). Both figures wear pleated *peploi*. The figure on the left holds the palm branch of victory over the bird and the other, on the right, is about to crown it with a wreath.

1. *L'DN LB'L 'MN [N] 'QYDŠ* [9]
2. *ND'R 'Š N'DR MTN*
3. *B'L BN B'LYTN PYG*
4. *'Š'M' 'T QWL' B'RK'* [10]

1) To the lord to Baal Amon the ?holy 2) a vow which vowed Muttun 3) baal son of Baalyaton dischar 4) ging his vow (because) he heard his voice (and) blessed him.

Presented by Sir Thomas Phillips, Bt., ex-Reade Collection
Bourgade 1852, 9, no. 8; Schröder 1869, 69 (NP 43); Chabot 1917a, 151, no. 10 (*Punica* 151-152); M'charek 1988, 744; Mendleson 1995, 261 and fig. 10.

NPu19. 125177 (57-12-18, 65)

32 x 38 x 14.5 cm

Fragment, well carved, in low relief. In the centre is a table with three cups, flanked on either side by a dolphin and cock. Traces of an upper register show a niche with the lower part of a column on the left and a fluted altar in the niche. On the outside of the niche is the bottom of a standard with a sunken circle with raised centre on the shaft. At the bottom of the fragment are traces of a panel with raised border which contained an inscription, the first few letters of which are visible.

L'DN L...

To the lord to...'

Bisi 1978, 42-3, and fig. 21

NPu20. 125079 (57-12-18, 61)

59 x 47 x 17 cm

Top of a worn stela. Within a rectangular frame with a rope border is a scene showing three deities. In the centre, in a gabled shrine with a bird at each corner, a beardless god sits on a stool. On the floor next to the stool are three small bowls, one above the other. He wears a *himation* which leaves the chest bare. In his right hand he holds up a large flat plate or mirror. The left arm extends into a damaged part of the stela. Flanking him are two standing goddesses. The goddess on his right wears a helmet and holds a spear in her right hand and a shield in her left (Athena). On his left another goddess holds a long spear or *thyrsus* in her left hand. She has long hair ending in two curls on her shoulders, reminiscent of the goddess Hathor. Her right hand is extended down toward the shrine and a bird at her feet. Just above her head there is another bird. Both goddesses wear *peploi*. In the field are two four-petalled rosettes with central bosses. Below this scene is a large shell.

Cf. Leglay 1961, pl. IX, 5 from Henchir Meded (Mididi).

NPu21. 125044 (S.O.C 56, 1880-1-30, 12)

53 x 32 x 5.8 cm

Middle section of a stela. A draped figure standing in a niche with rounded top holds two leafy standards outside the niche. The face is a circle, with basic features of eyes, nose and mouth damaged. No hair. Above is an inset panel with a four-line neo-Punic inscription. Above this is a circle framing a face with triangular rays (the sun). There is a countersunk circle on either side. The four-line inscription is a dedication to Baal Hammon by the citizens of Maktar.

1. *L'DN B'LḤMN K' ŠM'*
2. *QLM BRKM B'L' HMKT'RM*
3. *'TR 'RŠM BN MSYR'N W*
4. *Y'SKTN BN MSYGR'N*

1) To the lord Baal Hammon because he heard 2) their voices, he blessed them, the citizens (people) of Maktar 3) in the time of the suffetes Arisham son of Massiran and 4) Yaskatan son of Massigran.[11]

In the space at the end of lines 3 and 4 is a short inscription of three lines written in smaller letters. It reads

1. M'RWZ 2. 'BN B'L 3. ŠLK

1) Maruz 2) o, son of Baal 3) shillek

The additional inscription is considered by both Chabot and Sznycer to be a signature of the stone carver.

?1st century AD.

Found in 1833 by Sir Grenville Temple at Maghrawa near Maktar and presented to the Royal Asiatic Society and the India Museum in 1834.

Journal of the Royal Asiatic Society, 1 (1834), lxxxiii; Sir G. Temple, *Transactions of the Royal Asiatic Society, 3* (1835), 548-9 and pl. 23 (see App. 3); *Excursions in the Mediterranean* (London 1835) II, 344, pl. facing p. 358, no. 142 (and map facing p. 1) and 260-2; Gesenius 1837, 196-201; Ginsberg, *Script. Phoen. Monumment VII*; Bourgade 1852, 31, no. 9; Schröder 1869, 65 (NP 7), 264.1 and pl. XV,1; Chabot 1916a, 88-9 (*Punica*, 12-13); Bisi 1976, pl. I and p. 24-5; M'charek, *Actes IIIeme Congrès*, vol. II pl. 1, figs 1 and 2 for a similar stela from Maktar; Mendleson, *1995*, 258-9 fig. 1; M Sznycer, *Senitica 48,* (1999) for a full discussion of this stela.

Cf. Alaoui 1954, pl. CXXI, 1028; Bisi 1967, fig. 91; Phoenicians 1988, 168, for a similar stela, said to date to the 1st century BC.

NPu22. 125070 (59-4-2, 48)

45 x 28 x 13.5 cm

Stela fragment. A woman seated in a niche with rounded top within a shrine with horizontal lintel. The shrine has a triple recessed border. A fragment of coffered ceiling remains, supported by columns. The figure sits with hands in her lap wearing a full tunic with arm fastenings and a belt below the breasts. She wears round earrings and her hair is arranged in elaborate sausage curls. There are two countersunk circles with sunken centres in the niche and the shrine.

Bisi 1978, 31-2 and fig. 10

NPu23. 125073 (57-12-18, 64)

42 x 34.5 x 17.5 cm

Stela, top and bottom missing. In a niche with a rounded top is a female figure, possibly a goddess. She sits on a backless chair with carved arms and animal feet. On either side is a fluted column on a double base on the outside of which is a large palm frond. Below is a framed panel with concave sides containing two cult objects in low relief – a two-handled *amphoriskos* with pointed base next to a cylindrical box (*cista mystica*) with hatched top and bottom. Below this is a partly broken panel, also with concave sides, with roughened surface, possibly done to erase an inscription. The goddess sits with hands on her lap and holds a shallow bowl (*phiale*) in her right hand. She wears a tunic with chevron pleating across the top and fastenings on the right arm and shoulder. There is a narrow belt under the chest. The stylised folds at the bottom of the dress are depicted with a chevron design. A filmy mantle falls over her left shoulder.

Bisi 1976, 27, pl. IV,1 (wrongly numbered 125703).
Cf. NPu 24 for pedestal, hem of dress and right sleeve.

A note on stelae NPu 24–42

Though many of the following stelae, NPu 24-42, are fragmentary they have certain common characteristics. When complete they would have had three registers. The central register contains a figure with an offering standing in a niche within a shrine, the latter being depicted with much architectural detail, with columns or pilasters, bead and reel, dentil and ovolo mouldings and occasionally a coffered ceiling. Slight differences may be due to different workshops or to chronological development. NPu 24-28 are simpler and have less architectural detail – for example, the shrine does not have a pediment but only a simple vaulted roof – and these may be earlier. The shrines in NPu30-38 all have pediments with either a human head or a bird. In the field above the pediment an anthropomorphic nude female figure, a development of the so-called Tanit symbol, holds cornucopiae and fruit. Cupid, Dionysus and Venus may be shown standing on the pediment. The triangular top of the stela contains astral symbols such as a crescent and wreathed sun/moon or busts or faces of astral deities. Below the figure in the niche there is usually a sacrificial scene, or very rarely, a short inscription. On NPu29 the coffered ceiling appears on the floor and there is a neo-Punic dedication. The carving of NPu38 is naive but it has a Latin inscription, *RVSLM*, a dedication to a deity in fulfilment of a vow.

NPu24. 125043 (59-4-2, 42)

130.5 x 37 x 12 cm

Stela, top missing, but rough base still extant. In a niche with rounded arch a female figure stands on a pedestal with concave sides on which are shown a cylindrical wicker basket (*cista*) and possibly a double-handled libation vessel and ritual hammer (*malleus*). Her left hand is at her side and holds a round object (?apple). The right hand is bent in to her chest. She wears a long tunic with deep V-neck folded over her right arm and shoulder. A mantle covers her left shoulder. Her hair is arranged in sausage curls and she wears earrings and a necklace with a fishbone pattern and large round central pendant. The niche is part of a columned shrine with gabled roof. The legs of two figures (Venus and Dionysus) can be seen on either side of the pediment. Venus, on the left, rests her right hand on an altar with an incense cone; Dionysus, on the right, wears a *chlamys*. The shrine, niche and columns have countersunk holes and there are traces of similar holes in the field above the pediment. Below the niche is a male figure wearing a loincloth and holding a ritual knife, about to slaughter a bull. He wears a cap which shows some similarity to the caps on the men in a similar scene in NPu43.

Bisi 1978, 31 and fig. 9
Cf. NPu 23 for the pedestal with basket, hem of garment and right sleeve of cloak; Alaoui 1954, pls. CVI, no. 970, CIII, 966, from 'the Ghorfa'.

NPu25. 125192 (60-10-2, 120)

90.1 x 38 x 10.1 cm

Stela, gabled top and bottom missing. In a niche with rounded arch and fluted columns stands a female figure. She wears a pleated tunic and mantle which covers both arms. There is a bracelet on the slightly bent left arm. Her right arm is bent across her chest, palm up, and holds a round offering. Around her neck is a necklace with a central round pendant. The voussoirs of the arch have countersunk circles with central depressions. The same type of circle appears in rows in the field. On either side of the niche is a standard with three sunken circles with raised centres on the shafts; the finials have three leaves. Above the niche a large bird holds a round fruit in its beak. Above it a Tanit figure holds a cornucopia with clusters of grapes/dates in her right hand and a large pomegranate in her left at which two birds peck. Above is a fragment of the pediment with part of a crescent flanked by discs with sunken centres.

Cf. Alaoui 1954, pl. CIII, no. 965, for similar standards, clothes and columns, from 'the Ghorfa'.

NPu26. 125101 (57-12-18, 52)

100 x 39 x 15 cm

Stela, gabled top missing. A woman stands in a niche with rounded arch, her right hand on an altar, both on pedestals, that of the figure with concave sides. The woman wears tunic and mantle and a necklace with round central pendant. The voussoirs of the arch contain sunken circles and are supported by fluted columns. On either side of the niche is a standard with two concave circles with central holes on the shaft and a leaf emerging from the top. On the arch are two winged figures wearing *peploi*, one holding a large leafy branch, the other a wreath. Above this is a Tanit figure holding a large fruit cluster in her right hand and pomegranates in her left. Birds peck at the fruit. Over her head is a crescent with upturned ends and in one corner a sunken circle with raised centre. At the bottom of the stela are traces of another scene depicting two figures, one holding a wreath, the other a branch.

Bisi 1978, 36 and fig. 15
Cf. Alaoui 1954, pl. CIII, 965 from 'the Ghorfa'

NPu27. 125174 (59-4-2, 41)

74.4 x 32.5 x 15.5 cm

Gabled stela, bottom missing. In a niche with rounded top stands a female figure. She wears a tunic and a mantle which covers her shoulders and right arm; the left hand is extended, fist lightly clenched. Her right arm is bent in to the chest and holds a round offering, perhaps a pomegranate. Around her neck is a disc and crescent pendant, the crescent with upturned ends. Her elaborate hair-do has curls at the sides and a 'V' in the centre enclosing a small downward-pointing crescent. On either side of the niche is a standard whose shaft has three circles with central depression and raised border. On each standard is a bird which pecks at the fruit held by a Tanit figure standing over the niche. She holds a fruit cluster in her right hand and a pomegranate in her left. Birds peck at the fruit from above. In the pediment, which has a raised border, is a rosette and crescent, the crescent with upturned ends. Below these are three sunken circles.

Bisi 1978, 39 and fig. 17

NPu28. 125102 (59-4-2, 44)

67.5 x 38 x 18 cm

Upper part of gabled stela. In a round-arched niche supported on columns with crudely voluted capitals stands a man wearing a tunic and a mantle which covers his arms. In his right hand he holds a ?bird. He wears a necklace with round central pendant. On either side of the niche is a standard, of which only a part of one remains, with a sunken circle with central boss on the shaft and a finial of three leaves. Above the standard on either side of the niche is a wreathed, winged victory figure wearing a *peplos*. One holds a palm branch, the other a wreath. Above, a Tanit figure holds a cornucopia from which emerge a large fruit cluster and small pomegranate. In her other hand is a small fruit cluster and two large pomegranates. Birds peck at the fruit above and below. In the pediment, which is bordered by a double raised line, is a crescent with upturned ends flanked by libation bowls with long handles. Above all is a wreathed sun face.

Bisi 1978, 37-8 and fig. 16

NPu29. 125183 (57-12-18, 53 + 59-4-2, 38)

130.5 x 40; x 15.5 cm

Stela, only gabled top missing. In a niche with rounded arch is a male figure who stands on a high pedestal with concave sides and wears an enveloping mantle. Around his neck is a torque with a signet in the centre. He holds an offering in each hand. The right arm is bent to the chest while the left arm is at his side. His hair is arranged in short tight curls across the head. The niche is supported by two fluted columns and the voussoirs of the arch have countersunk circles with central depressions. On either side of the niche is a standard with wide base and two circles on the shaft. Below the niche is what appears to be a coffered ceiling, either a misunderstanding by the mason or an attempt to depict the ceiling in plan.[12] Above the niche two birds nibble beak to beak at a fruit cluster. Above them a Tanit figure holds a cornucopia with a large bunch of grapes/dates in her right hand and two pomegranates on a stalk in her left. Two birds peck at the grapes. At the top is a disc and crescent, the crescent with upturned ends and the disc with a round face enclosed in a wreath (moon and sun). On either side a bird holds a stem in its beak (perhaps the fruit from the scene below). They stand on a deeply carved ten-petalled rosette. In the field are inset circles with countersunk holes in the centre. At the bottom of the stela is a one-line inscription between two lightly traced lines.

1. N[D]'R 'Š N'D'R ŠM' QL' B'RK'

1) Vow which vowed for he heard his voice (and) blessed him.

Schröder 1869, 72 (NPu110); Chabot 1917b, 31-2 (*Punica*, 142-3 who reads [ND]R); Bisi 1978, 35-6 and fig. 14; Mendleson 1995, 261 and fig. 11.

NPu30. 125190 (59-4-2, 43)

113 x 38.5 x 14 cm

Stela, gable and lower part missing. A female figure stands in a round-arched niche in an elaborate temple facade. Her tunic covers her arms and she wears an enveloping mantle, one end of which is flung over her left shoulder. Her hair is dressed in sausage curls, a style typical of the Severan period. In her left hand she extends an oval offering; on the right arm, which is bent inwards at the waist, is a bracelet with an unusual motif. The temple has a horizontal lintel and recessed frame. Fluted columns with Ionic capitals support a coffered ceiling; the architrave has three decorative rows: dentils, bead and reel, and ovolo. In the gabled pediment, which has a raised border and bead and reel decoration, is a bearded male head. On the apex of the pediment is a large leaf from which spring two plants on stalks which look like dolphin tails but are probably meant to be cornucopiae. On the left of the pediment is a wreathed Dionysys wearing a *chlamys*. He holds a cup in his right hand and touches the central leaf with his left. On the right stands a nude Venus; her right hand is on the roof of the shrine, her left hand places a cone on an altar. A sunken circle with raised centre is in the field next to each figure. Above the shrine an anthropomorphic Tanit figure holds cornucopiae from which spring a large pomegranate and a grape/date cluster. She wears a rosette wreath. On either side of her head is a bird which pecks at a deeply carved six-pointed rosette/star. The rosettes flank a crescent with upturned ends and the remains of a circle (probably a sun face) framed in a wreath.

AD 180-200 or early 3rd century AD?
Leglay 1984, pl. IIIb; Bisi 1978, 23-4 and fig. 1..
Cf. Alaoui 1954, pl. CVIII, 974

NPu31.125186 (60-10-2, 119) +125075 (NPu43)

105.5 x 45-41 x ? cm
Gabled stela with a narrow raised border. Lower part missing. Below, only the head remains of a man standing in a niche with a round arch within a columned shrine. The columns have voluted capitals which support a coffered ceiling. The architrave has rows of dentil, bead and reel, and egg and dart moulding. The gabled shrine has a raised dentil border. In the centre of the pediment is a beardless male bust. Three figures stand on the pediment: on the apex is a naked bandy-legged winged Cupid. He holds a wreath in his left hand over an altar presided over by a nude Venus wearing only a thin necklace. With his right hand the Cupid clasps a *thyrsus* held by a cloaked Dionysus who holds a jug in his right hand. He wears a vine-branch wreath from which dangle fruit clusters. Above the group an anthropomorphic Tanit holds a cornucopia in her right hand from which spring a grape/date cluster and a pomegranate. In her left hand she holds a branch with two pomegranates. In the apex is a crescent with upturned ends and a wreathed sun face.

Leglay 1984, pl. IIIa; Bisi 1978, 26-7 and fig. 3.
Cf. Alaoui 1897, 62-3, nos. 741-752 (esp. no. 752) and pls. XVIII and XIX; Alaoui 1954, pls. CIV,967, CV,969.

Note: Since this catalogue was written, the stelae have been removed from exhibition and my colleague, Jonathan Tubb, noticed that the formerly missing lower part is in fact NPu43. This therefore now becomes one of the few complete neo-Punic stelae in the collection.

NPu32.125197 (57-12-18, 60)

60.5 x 37 x 12.5 cm
Stela fragment. A columned shrine with gabled roof within which is a niche with rounded arch. In the niche stands a man wearing a tunic and mantle which covers him completely except for his right arm which is bent in at the waist. His left arm is at his side. Flanking the niche are columns with voluted capitals. They support a coffered ceiling above which is an architrave with three decorative rows: dentils and two of bead and reel. In the pediment, which has a raised border, is a beardless male bust. On the pediment are a Cupid flanked by Dionysus and Venus as on NPu31. Venus presides over a horned altar and a bird rests on her arm.

Bisi 1978, 24-5 and fig. 2

NPu33.125072 (57-12-18, 54)

89 x 39.5 x 17 cm
Stela, central part only remaining. In a rounded niche within a shrine stands a woman wearing a tunic and a mantle which comes under the right arm and over the left shoulder and arm. In her extended left hand she holds a round object (?apple, *cf.* NPu24). Her right arm is bent in to her chest and holds a scroll (see NPu50 for similar offerings). She has sausage curls and round earrings and wears a necklace with a round central bead. Also in the niche is a small Nike in a *peplos* holding aloft a wreath. The columned shrine, with its voluted capitals, supports a coffered ceiling with dentils, ovolo, bead and reel and plain mouldings. In the pediment is a beardless male bust between two birds. The pediment has a raised dentil border. A nude Venus and a cloaked and wreathed Dionysus stand on the pediment. Dionysus holds a two-handled cup and a *thyrsus*. Venus has her left hand on a cone-topped altar on which stands a vulture. Her right hand holds a leaf of the stylised flower on the apex. Above the pediment is a Tanit figure, her garment filled with countersunk holes. She holds cornucopiae in each hand from which emerge fruit clusters, dates/grapes and a pomegranate. There are birds and countersunk holes in the field and countersunk holes surround the niche.

Goodenough, 138-9 and fig. 104; Bisi 1978, 34-5 and fig. 13 (incorrect BM number).
Cf. Alaoui 1897, pl. XIX, 746 and Alaoui 1954, pl. CIV, 967.

NPu34.125098 (57-12-18, 55)

131 x 35 x 13.5 cm
Stela, gable missing, unworked base remaining. A female figure stands on a high pedestal in a round-arched niche within a gabled shrine. Her extended left hand holds an offering. Her right hand is bent inwards to her chest. She wears a tunic and enveloping mantle and a double-stranded necklace. The shrine is supported by columns with voluted capitals; the architrave has dentils, ovolo, bead and reel and plain mouldings. The pediment has a triple recessed border; in the centre is a female head with streaming hair. On the left of the pediment is a bird and on the right a four-legged animal, apparently striped. On the apex is a nude, wreathed, female replacing the Tanit symbol. In each hand she holds a cone-shaped cornucopia from which emerge a palm tree and pomegranate on the left and a palm tree and grape/date cluster on the right. Below the pomegranate is a wreathed sun and above the figure are the remains of a crescent. Beneath the shrine is a bull *passant regardant*.

Bisi 1978, 30-1 and fig. 8.
Cf. Alaoui 1897, pl. XIX, 752 for similar head in pediment; *idem* 1954, pl. CVI, 970 for nude Tanit.

NPu35.125063 (57-12-18, 57)

81.5 x 38.5 x 17.5 cm
Gabled stela, lower part missing. The head of a man standing in a rounded niche within a gabled shrine remains as do the voluted capitals of the supporting columns. The niche has a flat roof and a triple recessed border. The architrave has rows of dentils, bead and reel, ovolo and rope mouldings separated by plain moulded rows, eight in all. In the pediment, which has a raised triple border with a bead

and reel row in the centre, a large bird with spread wings (either an eagle or a vulture), stands on a ball. On either side of the pediment stand two birds, a cock on the left and a ?dove on the right. On the apex stands a nude female on a pedestal, replacing Tanit. In her left hand she holds a cornucopia from which emerge two large bunches of dates/grapes; in her right hand is a branch with two pomegranates. Above her is an upturned crescent which encloses a deeply carved rosette. In the field are four countersunk circles.

Bisi 1978, 29 and fig. 7.
Cf. Alaoui 1954, pl. CVI, 970.

NPu36.125021 (57-12-18, 62)

58 x 25 x 11.5 cm
Upper part of gabled stela. Below, a male head is all that remains of a figure in the round-arched niche of a shrine. Voluted columns support a pediment with double border within which is a cock. Four plain bands form the architrave of the shrine. Above the pediment is a large Tanit figure holding cornucopiae from which emerge a large cluster of grapes/dates on one side and a pomegranate on the other. A bird pecks at the pomegranate. Above this, in the apex, is an upturned crescent surmounted by a rosette.

Bisi 1978, 27-8 and fig. 5.

NPu37.125184 (60-10-2, 121)

56 x 34 x 16 cm
Stela fragment. The head of a man in the niche of a columned shrine with voluted capitals. In the niche and around the rounded arch are holes, probably for affixing ribbons or streamers, or possibly for inlay. In the architrave are three rows of decorative moulding – dentils, bead and reel and ovolo. In the gabled pediment, which has a recessed double border, is a female bust with streaming hair and large hoop earrings. Standing on the point of the pediment is a damaged Tanit figure holding a cornucopia with a large cluster of grapes/dates in her right hand. Below the cluster, leaning on the pediment, is a wreathed Dionysus wearing a mantle covering one shoulder; grapes dangle from the wreath on either side of his head. On the other side of the pediment stands a nude Venus, also wreathed, holding another wreath in her right hand; her left hand rests on an altar.

Bisi 1978, 29 and fig. 6.
Cf. Alaoui 1897, pl. XIX, no. 752; *idem* 1954, pl. CVII, nos 972, 973.

NPu38.125189 ((60-10-2, 118)

123 x 34 x 12.5 cm
Stela, gable missing. A man stands in a rounded niche in a shrine. His right hand is bent inwards to his chest, while his left hand is at his side. He wears a tunic and enveloping mantle and has a torque around his neck. The shrine is supported by columns with voluted capitals. The architrave has plain, bead and reel, ovolo and dentil moulding above which is a pediment with triple border. Within the pediment is a four-leaved rosette with raised circles with countersunk centres between the leaves. Standing on the pediment are two figures: on the left is a cloaked Dionysus wearing a wreath and holding a cup in his right hand while in his raised left hand he holds a branch with fruit clusters emerging from the apex of the pediment; on the right is a chubby nude Venus with long straight hair, her left hand on an altar, her right hand also holding the fruit clusters. Above them is a Tanit figure (head missing) holding a large cluster of grapes/dates in each hand. Below all, in an inset rectangular panel, is a Latin inscription.

1. R.S.V.L.H.[13]

1) *Rogatus Solvit Votum Libens* H.

C.I.L. VIII, 1011; Poinssot 1905, 404-405; Bisi 1978, 22, n.3, p. 27 and fig. 4; J.P. Moore, 'Cultural Elasticity in the Inscription of the so-called "La Ghorfa" stelae, *AA* 35 (1999), 31-37.

NPu39.125104 (57-12-18, 66)

57 x 38.5 x 16 cm
Stela fragment, small portion of bottom part only. A coffered ceiling below a niche as in NPu 29. Below it is an animal, probably a lion, attacking a bull from the rear. This is a common Near Eastern motif occurring from the 3rd millennium onwards in many different materials.

Bisi 1978, 33 and fig. 11.

NPu40.125078 (59-4-2, 47)

50 x 43.5 x 16.5 cm
Top of stela, mainly pediment. Below is the apex of a shrine with a recessed border with dentil, bead and reel and plain moulding. At its apex are stylised flowers, one above the other. They support a Tanit figure with an upturned crescent on her head. She holds cornucopiae from which emerge clusters of dates/grapes on the left, and a pomegranate on the right. On one side of the pediment is a nude Venus holding a round offering. Also emerging from the pediment are branches with flowers. Above the crescent is a wreathed sun face with a deeply carved multi-petalled rosette on either side. In the field are two countersunk circles.

NPu41.125076 (57-12-18, 58)

79 x 40 x ? cm
Gabled stela, top only, in three registers separated by wreaths. In the pediment is a bearded male bust with right hand to his chest, palm out, holding a four-legged animal; a double wreath encloses his torso; a bird pecks at each ear. Flanking him are two small busts with human faces, one with rays (the sun), the other with horns (the moon). A deeply carved four-petalled flower is next to each bust and there is a larger eight-petalled rosette above the central figure. The dividing laurel wreath has a central countersunk circle. In the middle register an anthropomorphic Tanit holds cornucopiae from which emerge bunches of grapes/dates on the right and a cluster and pomegranate on the left. Two birds (?partridges) peck at the fruit. In the lower register is the gable of a shrine with a bead and reel border: in it stands a nude winged Cupid holding a fig or vine leaf in each hand; a bird pecks at each leaf. On his right, outside the pediment, on a pedestal stands a cloaked

Dionysus holding a *thyrsus* and two-handled cup; he wears a wreath with pendent clusters. Opposite and also on a pedestal stands a nude Venus, left hand on an altar, right hand outstretched holding a wreath. She wears anklets and a necklace with a central disc and crescent and a headdress of vine leaves. Below this the architrave of the missing shrine shows a row of ovolo moulding. Dotted around the stela are inset circles with deep centres, probably for additional ornamentation of ribbons or streamers.

c. 2nd century AD
Bisi 1978, 39-40 and fig. 18.
Cf. Alaoui 1897, pl. XIX, 748.

NPu42. 125062 (57-12-18, 63)

45 x 46.5 x 12.5 cm
Top of stela with small gable. In the pediment is a rayed head – the sun – flanked by double rosettes. A row of dentils separates the pediment from the register below which contains the top of a Tanit figure holding a cluster of grapes/dates in each hand. On each side is a palm tree beneath which stands a human figure. Above the Tanit is a horned head – the crescent moon – supported by two large stylised fish or dolphins. Flanking this and above the trees are two faces wreathed with snakes. All the faces have their hair parted in the centre except for the Tanit. In the field are groups of countersunk circles.

c.2nd century AD
Bisi 1978, 40 and fig. 19.
Cf. Alaoui 1897, pl. XVIII, 695 from Maktar.

NPu43. 125075 (57-12-18, 59) + 125186 (NPu31)[14]

71; x 45 x 16 cm
Stela fragment, which joins NPu 31 to form the complete stela. Standing in a columned niche is a figure wearing a full tunic and a mantle which covers the left shoulder and arm. It is probably a man and holds a ?cup in his left hand while placing an offering on a horned fluted altar with his right. Both stand on a pedestal with concave sides on which is written in Latin the name of a Roman citizen, 'L. *IULI URBA* (probably Lucius Iulius Urbanus) in *boustrephedon*. On either side of the columned niche is a larger column, no doubt supporting the shrine. Below is a scene of ritual sacrifice. On the left a priest wearing a belted tunic plays the twin Phrygian pipes.[15] In front of him is a similarly clad second priest in the act of killing a bull. He grasps the horn of the animal with a long hook in his left hand while with his right hand he is about to plunge a spear into the bull. Both humans are shown in crude profile with one round eye; both wear caps or masks which come down over the face and cover the nose. The bull's head faces forward; it is carefully carved and garlanded for sacrifice with a belt around its middle. The use of a spear rather than an axe indicates that this is not a dedication to Saturn.

There are no direct parallels but a number of stelae in the group said to be from the 'Ghorfa' show altars and bulls.

Bourgade 1852, 23, no. 36; Poinssot 1905, 403-404; Chabot 1917a, 165, no. 35 (*Punica*, 114); Leglay 1966, pl. II, 3; C.I.L VIII, 1145; Bisi 1978, 33 and fig. 12 (wrongly numbered 125705); Mendleson 1995, 261-2 and fig. 12; J.P. Moore, *AA*, 35 (1999) 35, and notes 24-25.
Cf. NPu 46.

NPu44. 125185 (60-10-2, 124)

60.5 x 32.7 x 12.2 cm
Gabled stela, top of pediment and bottom missing. The stela is in poor condition and the surface is flaking in a number of places. At the bottom is a rectangular frame in which are the remains of three lines of an illegible neo-Punic inscription. Above is a man standing in a shrine, his right hand resting on a fluted altar; he wears a full tunic and mantle. The shrine has fluted columns with thick bases and Ionic capitals with two rows of small holes; its roof is gabled and has a fleur-de-lys with two small holes at the apex. Flanking the shrine are standards with spear-shaped tips; each standard has two concave discs with central bosses on the shaft. Above the shrine, in the field at the sides, are two larger concave discs with central bosses, shields, libation bowls or possibly a symbol of office.

The stela has some unusual features: it has a neo-Punic inscription, the shrine is fairly plain and the background detail is comparatively restrained. Normally the masons tried to cover most of the surface whereas this one stands out in its simplicity. The spear-shaped standards flanking the shrine may indicate that the dedicant or the deceased was a military man.

Bisi 1976, pl. IV.2, p. 28, no. 8

NPu45. 125066 (59-4-2, 45+57-12-18, 56)

117 x 51 x 11.5 cm
Stela, top missing, three registers remaining. Above, badly worn, the Dioscuri, the horses with forepaws on a pedestal or altar on which stands Jupiter holding a staff (?thunderbolt), with an eagle. The scene is separated from the register below by a thick raised band. The middle register shows a woman standing in a niche within a shrine. She wears a full tunic and a mantle which covers her left arm and shoulder; her right hand is above a hexagonal altar while in her left is a shallow bowl. On either side of the niche is a narrow fluted column flanked by an upright leafy branch or palm frond. Supporting the shrine are fluted columns with elaborate capitals, the whole supporting an architrave consisting of a row of large discs. In the pediment, which has a double border, is a female head. On either side is a rosette with six petals. Tiny holes are drilled in these two registers, mainly in the centre. At the bottom of the stela two nude figures, between whom is a figure sacrificing a bull, support the shrine with upraised arms. Another figure stands behind the bull, holding it for sacrifice.

Leglay 1961, pl. VIII, 2 and p. 225; Bisi 1978, 41-2 and fig. 20.
Cf. Alaoui 1897, pl. XIX, 748, with a similar row of discs in the architrave.

NPu46. 125115 (50-3-4, 42)

66 x 33 x 8.5 cm
Stela with three registers. Above, a bearded deity (Saturn) sits on a stool. He wears a *himation* which leaves his chest bare. His right hand holds a ?pruning knife on his lap and his left arm is raised behind his ear, perhaps holding a veil. On his left shoulder is a rosette. Flanking him are the Dioscuri, holding prancing horses.

In the central register a female figure stands in a niche with rounded ceiling which sports lotus flower embellishments. She stands beside a hexagonal altar, on a narrow platform, her right hand over the flames, in the act of offering incense. In her left hand is a basket with a loop handle, probably containing incense. She wears a long sleeveless tunic (*chiton*), fastened in three places on her right shoulder and arm, and a mantle. Around her chest is a belt tied with a 'knot of Hercules'. Her hair is dressed in large sausage curls shaped closely around her head. Flanking the niche are two large Corinthian columns supporting a flat lintel with dentils.

In the bottom register two nude kneeling Atlas figures support the shrine on their backs. They flank a man wearing a short tunic who is giving the *coup de grâce* to a bull.

Reade Collection
Winstanley 1850, lot 43; Leglay 1961, pl. VIII, 1 and p 224; Amiet *et al.*, *Art in the Ancient World,* (London, 1981) 500, no. 69.
Cf. Gauckler *et al.*, *Cat. du Musée Alaoui*, Supplément (Paris 1910), pl. LI, 1 and p. 64, no. 1098.

NPu47.125200 (57-12-18,67)

28 x 38 x 13 cm
Stela fragment. Two bearded Atlas figures, not kneeling but appearing to be seated. They support a shrine which has a row of bead and reel decoration. Above are the damaged remains of a bull. At the side is a palm frond.

NPu48.125178 (50-3-4, 36)

59.5 x 29 x 6 cm
Small stela which has been recut and reshaped. In a flat-topped niche stands a female figure holding a sheaf of wheat or corn ears in her left hand and a shallow bowl in her right. She wears a calf-length tunic with a V-neck. A short cloak covers her upper body and falls over her left shoulder, ending in a tassel. On either side of the niche is a carved panel with listels and a vertical double leaf design. The top of the stela has been recut and there is a large hole in the centre.

Late 2nd century (AD 180-200)
Reade Collection
Bisi 1976, pl. III.2, pp. 26-7

NPu49.125180 (50-3-4, 37)

78 x 30 x 9.5 cm
Stela, apex and base missing. A man with tiny arms stands in a shrine. He wears a striped or pleated calf-length tunic. In his left hand he holds an incised caduceus; his right arm is bent inwards to his chest and he holds or wears a breastplate or *insignium*. The shrine has a flat roof with a row of dentil moulding and is supported by columns. The pediment, which is sharply gabled with stylised acroteria, has a dentil border within which is an eagle with outstretched wings. Between the pediment and acroteria are stylised trees, of which the one on the right may be a palm. Standing on the tree on the left are a bird and a goat, while on the right is a bull. Between them is the stem of a stylised flower supporting a sun symbol from around which emerge three running feet (a *triquetra*). The bottom foot holds the flower symbol on the pediment. The left foot holds a branch at which a bird pecks, the right foot a pomegranate. Above, in the field, are the remains of a rosette.

2nd century AD
Reade Collection
Winstanley 1850, lot 38; Bisi 1978, 22-3 and fig. 22
Cf. Alaoui 1954, pl. XCVIII, 939 for tree and animals from Ain Barchouch

NPu50.125179 (50-3-4,44)

42 x 32 x 13 cm
Stela fragment. In a niche with slightly rounded top stands a woman with her right leg slightly forward. She wears a long tunic and a mantle covers her right arm and shoulder. The hem of the tunic folds in a chevron pattern. Her right arm is bent in at the waist and holds an offering (?scroll or wheatsheaf); her left hand is extended, holding open the mantle and at least two other offerings. The face is carefully shown with the pupils of the eyes carved, and her hair is arranged in large sausage curls. There are two deep holes on either side of the head, probably for the insertion of ribbons or other organic material. This may be a tombstone.

AD 180-200
Reade Collection
Winstanley 1850, lot 45 (not illustrated)
Cf. for scroll Alaoui 1954, pls. CVI, 970, CXIII, 995.

NPu51.125106 (59-4-2, 46)

51 x 39 x 16.5 cm
Stela fragment. A woman stands in a niche with a flat ceiling and plain moulded rows in the architrave. She wears a full tunic and mantle with stylised folds and holds a ?scroll in her right hand. The face and hair are carefully shown, with the pupils of the eyes indicated by incised circles. The stela is broken from the waist down. There was originally another figure on her right but the only remaining traces are the outline of a head. Above the niche, in what was the pediment, is a reclining male figure with a full leonine beard. He wears a cloak which leaves his chest and right arm and shoulder bare, right hand held to his head, a rather crude depiction of Saturn. Next to him is a damaged figure.

Bisi 1976, pl. v,1 and pp. 28-9.

NPu52.125116 (50-3-4, 43)

52 x 32 x 6 cm
Stela, middle section only. A woman standing in a niche. Square pilasters with Corinthian capitals support an architrave with a row of dentil and a row of ovolo moulding. The woman wears a full tunic with shoulder stripes (*clavi*) and a mantle with a rolled upper edge. She wears two necklaces, one with beads and a large central bead, the other consisting of trapezoidal plaques again with a large central round bead. She stands by a flaming horned altar on which she places incense from a small box or casket held in her left hand. Above the niche is a register with the head of a deity (Saturn), with stylised ornately curled beard and hair and incised eye pupils. On his right is a series of three symbols, one above the other. At the bottom is a lidded basket or casket, no doubt a *cista mystica*, then two circles with incised centres, and above that a *falx*, the knife used for cutting

vines. On the other side of the head, in the upper corner, is a filled cornucopia.

Late 2nd century AD
Reade Collection
Winstanley 1850, lot 44; Leglay 1961, pl. VIII,3 and p. 225 (who considers it to be 3rd century AD); Bisi 1976, no. 10, p. 29, pl.V,2.

NPu53.125176 (50-3-4,41)

94 x 51 x 13.5 cm

Stela in three registers. Above is a reclining bearded male figure (Saturn), weight on his left elbow, hand at his head, the other arm lying along his side. He wears a skirt which leaves the torso bare. The face is crudely but carefully carved with holes for the eye pupils; hair and beard are dressed in short curls and a veil covers his head and comes down to the shoulders. Behind him, two male figures in military dress hold horses whose front hooves rest on pedestals (the Dioscuri). The centre register depicts a man and woman standing on either side of an altar. The man wears a tunic and toga, the woman a full tunic and mantle with decorated upper edge. The man places a round offering on the altar and holds in his left hand a casket with gabled lid. The woman holds a cylindrical box or offering in both hands. The bottom register depicts a man in a *chlamys* leading a bull to an altar. On the right of the altar another figure holds on his head a large basket with a gabled lid. There are drilled holes around the border and in the field, for metal or textile insertions.

c. 3rd century AD
Reade Collection
Winstanley 1850, lot 42; Leglay 1961, pl.VIII, 4 and p. 225-6;
Cf. Alaoui 1897, pl. XX, no. 753 from El-Lehs

NPu54.125181 (50-3-4, 40)

100 x 53 x 12.5 cm

Stela, two registers and base remaining. Below, a man leads a bull to an altar. On the other side of the altar a small figure carries on his head a basket with a gabled lid. The top register shows two couples, each couple standing before an altar. The women wear tunics and mantles with broad decorated bands; the men wear tunics and togas. All the figures hold offerings. There are three holes around each head and holes in the border of the top register.

?3rd century AD
Reade Collection
Winstanley 1850, lot 41; Leglay 1961, 226, 8 (not illustrated) who considers it to be 2nd century AD.

NPu55.125077 (50-3-4, 39)

74 x 43 x 10 cm

Stela, flat top, three registers. Above, a bearded deity (Saturn) stands in the centre. He holds a *falx* in his right hand and his left hand is raised to his head. He is flanked by the Dioscuri with horses. In the central register, which has a double arch, a man and woman stand on either side of a horned altar on a tapering base. The woman wears a tunic with *clavi* and short veil and the man also wears a tunic with *clavi* and a mantle. The folds of the garments of both figures are highly stylised. They each hold an offering and have one hand on the altar. Below is a man with a bull and, on its other side, a man holding a gabled basket on his head. All the eyes of the figures have incised holes and there are larger holes on the border.

Late 3rd-early 4th century AD
Reade Collection
Winstanley 1850, lot 40; Leglay 1961, pl. VIII,6 and p. 226.
Cf. Alaoui 1897, pl. XX, no. 753 from El-Lehs.

NPu56.125345(50-3-4-,38)

81 x 43.5 x 9.5 cm

Stela with flat top. Four registers. Above stands a bearded deity (Saturn) holding a *falx* in his right hand with his left arm raised to his head. He wears a *himation* which leaves his chest bare. The bottom part of his body goes down into the register below. He is flanked by the Dioscuri who wear belted tunics; their horses face foward. Below this a man and woman stand in arches on either side of an altar, holding offerings, one hand over the altar. A large basket sits on the floor beside the woman who wears a stylised sleeved tunic and short mantle. The man also wears a stylised sleeved tunic and a mantle which comes across the waist and over his left arm. Below is a man holding a bull. He wears a long belted tunic and holds a staff or cattle prod. On the other side of the bull is a figure wearing a long robe with a large basket on his head. In the bottom register are three supporting figures facing front. The eyes of all the figures are incised. There are holes at various places on the border and beneath the figure of Saturn.

Late 3rd–early 4th century AD
Reade Collection
Winstanley 1850, lot 39; Leglay 1961, pl.VIII,5 and p. 226; E. Kitzinger, *Early Medieval Art* (London, 1969), pl. 2, 9,99.
Cf. Alaoui 1897, pl. XX, no. 753, from El-Lehs

NPu57.125191 (57-12-18, 39)

105 x 29 x 17 cm

Tombstone with gabled top. In the centre a male figure stands in a deeply recessed niche with rounded top. He wears a long tunic and a mantle which falls over his left shoulder. His left arm is at his side; the right is bent, palm in, to his chest. The face is blank and appears never to have been carved. Above the niche, in the apex, is a six-petalled rosette below which is an altar from which emerge two large bunches of grapes/dates. Below the niche, in an inset rectangular panel with concave sides, is a three-line neo-Punic inscription.

1. *ṬN' 'BN Z LPLKS BN*
2. *P'WST' WKN ŠNT ŠLŠ*
3. *TM B'YM*

1) This stone has been set up for Felix, son of 2) Faustus: and he was three years 3) honourably in life.

Bourgade 1852, 19, no. 24; Schröder 1869, 69 (NP 58); Lidzbarski 1898, 436, no. 4, pl. XX.3; Chabot 1916b, 453 (*Punica*, 43); Bisi 1976, pl. III.1 and p. 25; WAI 134.

NPu58.125193 (60-10-2, 117)

105 x 34.5 x 17 cm

Tombstone, complete, with rounded top and two small acroteria. Within a niche with rounded top stands a female figure, right hand to her chest. She wears a finely pleated tunic and a mantle which covers her left arm. The wide tunic covers her right arm. Her hair is dressed in sausage curls and she wears pendant earrings and a necklace with a large round central bead. Below the figure, in a square inset panel is a four-line Latin inscription, on ruled lines.

1. *MAXIMILLA.*
2. *BASSI. F PIA*
3. *VIX. AN. XIX*
4. *H S E.*

1) Maximilla 2) pious daughter of Bassi, 3) lived 19 years. 4) Here she is placed (*Hic sita est*).

C.I.L. VIII, no. 1052; Bisi 1976, pl. II,2 and p. 26

NPu59. 125175 (57-12-18, 40)

95 x 37 x 13.4 cm

Tombstone with rounded top, slightly damaged. In a round-arched niche stands a female figure (face damaged), left hand at her side, the other bent in with open palm to the chest. She wears a wide tunic which covers her right arm and an enveloping mantle. Below, in an inset panel, is a four-line neo-Punic inscription.

1. *Ṭ‘’N Z LBRK‘L*[16]
2. *BT Y‘ŠDBY*
3. *W‘W‘ Š‘NT*[17]
4. *’SRM W‘MŠ*

1) This was set up for Barak‘l/ Barak<ba>al 2) daughter of Yashdibi[18] 3) and she lived 4) 25 years.

1st century AD
Bourgade 1852, 18, no. 16; Schröder 1869, 69, 270.10, pl. XVII.11 (NP 51); Lidzbarski 1898, 436, no. 7, pl. XX,7; Chabot 1917a, 155, no. 18 (*Punica*, 104); Bisi 1976, pl. 1,2 and p. 25.
Cf. Picard 1957, pl. XIII.

NPu60. 125099 (57-12-18, 41)

113 x 40 x 17.5 cm

Gabled tombstone. Rough surface except for the simple decoration. A central niche with rounded top contains a bust. Below, in an inset rectangular panel, is a three-line neo-Punic funerary inscription:

1. *ṬN’ ‘BN Z LG’ML’ BN*
2. *SHLDY’ ‘W’ Š‘NT*
3. *ḤMŠM*

1) This (tomb)stone has been set up for Gemellus, son of 2) Selidius. He lived 3) 50 years

Bourgade 1852, 18, no. 18; Schröder 1869, 69 (NPu53); Chabot 1917a, 157, no. 20 (*Punica*, 106 no. 20); Bisi 1976, pl. II,1 and p. 26; KAI 135.

NPu61. 125095 (59-4-2, 40)

51 x 21 x 16 cm

Tombstone, top damaged. Three-line neo-Punic inscription only with a fourth line having the Roman numerals XXX.

1. *ṬN’ ’BN Z L*
2. *ṬṬY‘ BT*
3. *KLNY BT ŠNT*
4. *XXX*

1) This stone was set up for 2) Titia daughter of 3) Clonius, aged 4) 30.
The ‘30' is in Roman numerals.

Levy, *Phon. Stud* III, p. 64, no. 2 ; Schröder 1869, 72 (NPu117); Chabot 1917b, 35, no. 8 (*Punica*, 146-7).

Notes

1 See Brown 1991, no. 510.
2 For MSQY: Jongeling 1984, 184, propose Latin Messucius (*cf.* probably CIL VIII 6632). There are also Berber names of the type Mazic, Masisic, etc. see Jongeling 1994, 90. Chabot also proposed Messucius. For QRTLY Chabot and Jongeling proposed Cartilius, for KST’, Cestius.
3 The vowels are not sure at all; this could be a Berber name .
4 Here too the vowels are not sure. *Cf.* Thusabiae, gen..., *Karthago* VII, 1957, 77; Jongeling 1994, 142.
5 This reading is very tentative; it could be *MSPRDT* or *MSPNDT*. G is not sure because it can be formed partly by the L of *‘BDM[L]QRT*. The Chabot reading (uncertain) is *MŠ PRD‘N.* Jongeling 1994, 200 accepts *PRD‘N.*
6 *Y‘L SS‘N* and *BŠTS‘N* appear to be Numidian names and their vocalisation is uncertain.
7 Chabot 1917a reads *KḤT* and considers the repetition of the word as a form of intensity of meaning.
8 The second letter seems to be *Š* – a mistake for ‘.
9 *’QYDŠ* is probably a late orthography for *HQDŠ*. *Y* is perhaps the result of a regressive vowel assimilation (*qadiš> qidiš). See Hoftizer-Jongeling 99b.
10 Vowels have been inserted in the text so that the vocalization is better understood. Ḥ has been replaced by an ‘, as has the *aleph* in Adon.
11 The vowels of the Berber names are conventional. Jongeling registers in Latin letters: Iasuctan, Masiran (in a Latino-Punic inscription: *IRTS* 20, 138; p. 13 Jongeling cites Lib. MSIGRN as an equivalent of MSYGR‘N: s. *RIL*, nos 545, 641. For M‘RWZ *cf.* perhaps MRS. RIL, no. 108
12 This is not unique. There is a very similar stela in the Louvre (Bisi 1978, 57, fig. 25), where the coffered ceiling is below the niche. The fragment NPu38 was also part of a similar stela.
13 The inscription is probably meant to read *RVSLM* for *VOTUM SOLVIT LIBENS MERITO*, ‘Rogatus gladly/willingly redeems his vow deservedly.’ C.I.L. interprets it as *Rogatus votum solvit libens animo* and considers the ‘H’ letter to be a mason’s error.
14 See NPu31.
15 The Phrygian pipes were brought to Rome by priests of the cult of the Asiatic mother goddess Cybele in 204 BC. Her cult never became completely Roman and citizens were not allowed to participate in its ceremonies or to wear its peculiar dress. However, the musical instruments used in the cult became popular. It is known that Cybele was worshipped in North Africa: a temple dedicated to the goddess in 71/2 AD has been found at Lepcis Magna (Mackendrick 1980, 148) and inscriptions to her were found at Caesarea in Mauretania (Mackendrick 1980, 207).
16 Perhaps the stone mason meant to write: *Ṭ‘<N’> ’<B>N Z LBRK<B>‘L.*
17 The stone mason has written *Š‘LT* instead of ŠNT
18 Yashdibi is conventional. Jongeling 1994, 63 gives IASIDBA [CIL VIII 11434], perhaps Berber.

Personal Names

The true pronounciation of many of the names below is uncertain. The author has based these transliterations mainly on a combination of traditional renderings and Hebrew parallels, also taking into consideration the Latin forms of some of the names (which may have become corrupted over time). For example, in the case of names composed with Melqart, it may be that the Phoenician form was Milqart, i.e. the Latin names, Hamilcar and Bomilcar. Another traditional transliteration is in the pronounciation of TNT which we have kept as the traditional 'Tanit' but is now thought to have been Tinnit.

Punic

'BNB'L	?Abnbaal	Pu87
'BRKT (f)	Aberkat/?Aberkot	Pu32
'DNB'L	Adonibaal	Pu48, Pu54, Pu86, ?Pu87, Pu88, Pu115
'DRB'L	Addirbaal	Pu47
'M'ŠTRT (f)	Am'ashtart	Pu70
'MTMLQRT(f)	Amotmelqart	Pu6
'RŠ	Arish	Pu15, Pu29, Pu46
'RŠM	Arisham	Pu7, Pu76
'RŠT (f)	Arishat [Lat. Arisuth(h), Arist]	Pu65, Pu77, Pu95
'ŠMNḤLṢ	Eshmunhilles [Eshmunahalos]	Pu57, Pu73
'ŠMNYTN	Eshmunyaton	Pu46
'ŠMNŠMR	Eshmunshamar [Eshmunshamor]	Pu10
BD'	Bodo	Pu11, Pu53
BD'ŠMN	Bodeshmun	Pu7, Pu43, Pu82
BDMLQRT	Bodmelqart	Pu2, Pu13, Pu17, Pu22, ?Pu32, Pu37, Pu39, Pu51, Pu54, Pu55, 60, Pu71, Pu81, Pu83, Pu84, Pu85, Pu86, Pu90, Pu91
BD'ŠTRT	Bod'ashtart	Pu7, Pu10, Pu12, Pu36, Pu39, Pu52, ?Pu67, Pu68, Pu75, Pu77, Pu78, Pu87, Pu88, Pu89, Pu106, Pu116
B'LḤLṢ	Baalhilles	Pu91
B'LḤN'	Baalhanno	Pu18, Pu69, Pu83, Pu90, Pu106, Pu116
B'LYTN	Baalyaton	Pu51, Pu61, ?Pu63, Pu65, Pu92
B'LML'K	Baalmalok	Pu79
B'L'ZR	Baal'azor	Pu77, Pu112
B'L'LK	Baalillek	Pu93
B'LŠLK	Baalshillek	Pu34, Pu38, Pu72, Pu93, Pu108
B'LŠPT	Baalshafot	Pu88
BTB'L (f)	Batbaal	Pu56, Pu94
GDN'M (f)	Gadna'am	Pu95
GRSKN	Gersakon	Pu75, Pu84, Pu99, Pu109
GR'ŠTRT	Ger'ashtart	Pu34, Pu55, ?Pu67, Pu75, Pu115
ZBG	?Zabog	Pu92
ZYWG	?Ziwag	Pu96
ḤLṢB'L	Hillesbaal [Halosbaal]	Pu85
ḤMLK	Himilk	Pu69
ḤMLKT	Himilkot	Pu2, Pu18, Pu30, Pu31, Pu34, Pu37, Pu39, Pu53, Pu57, Pu69, Pu71, Pu78, Pu79, Pu117
ḤMLQRT	Himilqart	Pu108

ḤN'	Hanno	Pu3, Pu12. Pu13, Pu16, Pu30, Pu36, Pu46, Pu51, Pu52, Pu68,Pu79, Pu80, Pu81, Pu95
ḤNB'L	Hannibaal	Pu40, Pu48, Pu53, Pu79, Pu89, Pu111
ḤTMLKT	Hotmilkot	Pu66
YḤNB'L	Yahonbaal	Pu75
YḤW'	?Yahua	Pu32
?YKNSHALIM	Yakonshalim	Pu19
YTNT	?Yatanit	Pu33
YTNB'L	Yatonbaal	Pu100
KBDT (f)	Kabdot	Pu97
LBT (f)	Labot	Pu23
MGN	Magon	Pu3, Pu13, Pu14, Pu18, Pu41, Pu66, Pu81, Pu95
MHRB'L	Maharbaal	Pu16, Pu56, Pu78, Pu98, Pu101, Pu111
MTN'LM	Muttunelim	Pu1
MTNB'L (f)	Muttunbaal	Pu99, Pu100
MLKYTN	Milkyaton	Pu84, Pu101
MLQRTḤLṢ	Melqarthilles [Milqarthalos?]	Pu90
NBG	?Nabag	Pu102
NML	?Namal	Pu93
'BD	'Abd(o)	Pu20
'BD'	'Abdo	Pu19, Pu29, Pu97
'BDMLK	'Abdmilk	?Pu23, Pu33
'BDMLQRT	'Abdmelqart	Pu12, Pu17, Pu23, Pu31, Pu32, ?Pu34, Pu38, Pu49, Pu68, Pu71, Pu76, Pu77, Pu58, Pu92, Pu103, Pu108, Pu109, Pu110
'BD'ŠMN	Abdeshmun	Pu11, Pu22, Pu31, Pu36, ?Pu40, Pu41, Pu60, Pu82, Pu103, Pu104, Pu105, Pu106, Pu107, Pu109
'BDTNT	'Abdtanit	Pu104
'BRGH	?'Abergoh	Pu70
'MTB'L (f)	'Amotbaal	Pu35
'ZMLK	'Azmilk	Pu110
'ZR	'Azor	Pu97
'ZRB'L	'Azrubaal	Pu2, Pu11, Pu14, Pu33, Pu54, Pu55, Pu75, Pu108, Pu111, Pu115
'KBR	'Akbor	Pu29, Pu48, Pu72, Pu80
'LŠT (f)	?'Alshat	Pu112
'ŠTRTYTN	'Ashtartyaton	Pu10
PDY	Pady	Pu30
PRŠ	?Parosh	Pu102
ṢLḤ	Selah	Pu105
ŠPT	Shafot	Pu43, Pu75
ŠṢP	?Shasaf	Pu1

Neo-Punic

’DNB‘L	Adonibaal	NPu2, NPu11
’DRB‘L	Addirbaal	NPu2
’RŠ	Arish	NPu2
’RŠM	Arisham	NPu21
BDB‘L	Bodbaal	NPu15
B‘L’NG (f)	?Baaloneg	NPu6, NPu9
B‘LYTN	Baalyaton	NPu18
B‘LŠLK	Baalshillek	NPu21
B‘NK	?Banok	NPu9
BRKB‘L	Barikbaal	NPu10, NPu59
BRK‘L (f)	Barakel	NPu59
ḤMLK	Himilk	NPu3
ḤN’	Hanno	NPu1
ḤNB‘L	Hannibaal	NPu6
MTN	Muttun	NPu17
MTNB‘L	Muttunbaal	NPu1, NPu3, NPu18
MTNHYB‘L(f)	Muttunhibaal	NPu14
‘BDMLQRT	‘Abdmilqart	NPu6, NPu8, NPu11, NPu17
‘ZRB‘L	‘Azrubaal	NPu3, NPu13
ŠYPK (f)	?Shipak	NPu7

Latin

Clonius	NPu61
?Cornutus	NPu15
CRES	NPu4
Faustus	NPu57
Felix	NPu57
Gaius Iulius Arish	NPu2
Gemellus	NPu60
L. Iulius Urba	NPu43
Maximilla Bassi (f)	NPu58
Cartilius Cestius	NPu5
Rogatus	NPu38
Titia	NPu61

Others

BŠTS‘N	NPu10
HBKTYZ‘	NPu12
YLGM	NPu13
Y‘SKTN	NPu21
Y‘LṢS‘N	NPu10
Y‘ŠDBY	NPu59
MSYGR‘N	NPu21
MSYR‘N	NPu21
M‘KL’	NPu12
M‘RWZ	NPu21
MṢQY	NPu5
MŠNGD‘T?	NPu8
SHLDY’/Selidiu	NPu60
TZ‘BŠ	NPu7

Concordances of Numbers

Museum numbers and catalogue numbers

Punic

125071	TM 1	125235	Pu107	125278	Pu82
125171	TM 2	125236	Pu92	125279	Pu8
125182	TM 8	125237	Pu52	125280	Pu49
125187	TM 3	125238	Pu51	125281	Pu73
125188	TM 4	125239	Pu3	125282	Pu47
125199	TM 5	125240	Pu86	125283	Pu90
125317	TM 7	125241	Pu109	125284	Pu27
125319	TM 6	125242	Pu87	125285	Pu31
		125243	Pu111	125286	Pu29
118787	Pu6a	125244	Pu5	125287	Pu38
125083	Pu67	125246	Pu84	125288	Pu94
125084	Pu4	125247	Pu44	125289	Pu61
125085	Pu53	125248	Pu35	125290	Pu103
125086	Pu83	125249	Pu56	125291	Pu48
125087	Pu57	125250	Pu63	125292	Pu66
125088	Pu39	125251	Pu30	125293	Pu7
125089	Pu42	125252	Pu2	125294	Pu117
125091	Pu1	125253	Pu20	125295	Pu33
125208	Pu41	125254	Pu34	125296	Pu102
125209	Pu13	125255	Pu96	125297	Pu77
125210	Pu9	125256	Pu70	125298	Pu80
125211	Pu17	125257	Pu106	125299	Pu36
125212	Pu85	125258	Pu11	125300	Pu59
125213	Pu89	125259	Pu79	125301	Pu104
125214	Pu88	125260	Pu10	125302	Pu78
125215	Pu112	125261	Pu6	125303	Pu74
125216	Pu26	125262	Pu95	125304	Pu40
125217	Pu72	125263	Pu75	125305	Pu60
125218	Pu93	125264	Pu37	125306	Pu99
125220	Pu101	125265	Pu58	125307	Pu65
125221	Pu19	125266	Pu69	125308	Pu15
125222	Pu62	125267	Pu22	125309	Pu76
125223	Pu54	125268	Pu91	125310	Pu115
125224	Pu18	125269	Pu46	125311	Pu21
125227	Pu64	125270	Pu113	125312	Pu98
125228	Pu24	125271	Pu28	125313	Pu110
125229	Pu108	125272	Pu50	125314	Pu97
125230	Pu23	125273	Pu105	125323	Pu14
125231	Pu100	125274	Pu114	125324	Pu71
125232	Pu25	125275	Pu116	125330	Pu81
125233	Pu45	125276	Pu12	125718	Pu43
125234	Pu55	125277	Pu32	125719	Pu68
				135693	Pu16

Neo-Punic

125021	NPu36	125095	NPu61	125179	NPu50
125043	NPu24	125098	NPu34	125180	NPu49
125044	NPu21	125099	NPu60	125181	NPu54
125045	NPu10	125100	NPu3	125183	NPu29
125050	NPu8	125101	NPu26	125184	NPu37
125056	NPu1	125102	NPu28	125185	NPu44
125057	NPu11	125103	NPu16	125186	NPu31
125062	NPu42	125104	NPu39	125189	NPu38
125063	NPu35	125105	NPu6	125190	NPu30
125066	NPu45	125106	NPu51	125191	NPu57
125069	NPu4	125115	NPu46	125192	NPu25
125070	NPu22	125116	NPu52	125193	NPu58
125072	NPu33	125117	NPu2	125194	NPu9
125073	NPu23	125118	NPu12	125195	NPu5
125075	NPu43	125119	NPu15	125196	NPu7
125076	NPu41	125174	NPu27	125197	NPu32
125077	NPu55	125175	NPu59	125198	NPu13
125078	NPu40	125176	NPu53	125200	NPu47
125079	NPu20	125177	NPu19	125345	NPu56
125090	NPu18	125178	NPu48	125981	NPu14
				136681	NPu17

Departmental and Registration numbers and list of inscriptions

Tomb Markers *(8)*

125071	60-10-2, 123
125171	57-12-18, 74
125182	57-12-18, 68
125187	57-12-18, 70
125188	57-12-18, 71
125199	57-12-18, 73
125317	57-12-18, 72
125319	57-12-18, 69

Punic Stelae *(118)*

118787	1927-9-22, 1	
125083	59-4-2, 25	inscription
125084	60-10-2, 3	inscription
125085	57-12-18, 8	inscription
125086	59-4-2, 4	inscription
125087	59-4-2, 34	inscription
125088	57-12-18, 10	inscription
125089	S.O.C. 100	
125091	S.O.C. 102	inscription
125208	86-6-21, 5	inscription
125209	57-12-18, 27	inscription
125210	59-4-2, 9	inscription
125211	60-10-2, 7	inscription
125212	57-12-18, 16	inscription
125213	60-10-2, 15	inscription
125214	57-12-18, 28	inscription
125215	57-12-18, 32	inscription
125216	57-12-18, 79	
125217	59-4-2, 35	inscription
125218	76-2-25, 4	inscription
125220	59-4-2, 32	inscription
125221	59-4-2, 23	inscription
125222	57-12-18, 81	
125223	59-4-2, 24	inscription
125224	86-6-21, 4	inscription
125227	57-12-18, 26	inscription
125228	57-12-18, 78	
125229	59-4-2, 18	inscription
125230	57-12-18, 17	inscription
125231	59-4-2, 26	inscription
125232	57-12-18, 75	
125233	57-12-18, 83	
125234	59-4-2, 27	inscription
125235	59-4-2, 8	inscription
125236	59-4-2,31	inscription
125237	57-12-18, 23	inscription
125238	57-12-18, 12	inscription
125239	57-12-18, 3	inscription
125240	57-12-18, 51	inscription
125241	59-4-2, 29	inscription
125242	57-12-18, 18	inscription
125243	59-4-2, 19	inscription
125244 + 125245	57-12-18, 77	
125245	57-12-18, 82	
125246	57-12-18, 31	inscription
125247	57-12-18, 76	

125248	59-4-2, 16	inscription
125249	57-12-18, 20	inscription
125250	76-3-11, 1	inscription
125251	59-4-2, 14	inscription
125252	86-6-21, 6	inscription
125253	76-2-25, 3	inscription
125254	57-12-18, 14	inscription
125255	59-4-2,2	inscription
125256	57-12-18, 6	inscription
125257	59-4-2, 17	inscription
125258	86-6-21, 1	inscription
125259	59-4-2, 1	inscription
125260	57-12-18, 2	inscription
125261	57-12-18, 30	inscription
125262	57-12-18, 36	inscription
125263	76-2-25, 8	inscription
125264	57-12-18, 35	inscription
125265	76-2-25, 1	inscription
125266	59-4-2, 33	inscription
125267	57-12-18, 29	inscription
125268	60-10-2, 12	inscription
125269	57-12-18, 5	inscription
125270	57-12-18, 34	inscription
125271	76-2-25, 2	
125272	57-12-18, 1	inscription
125273	60-10-2, 8	inscription
125274	60-10-2, 9	inscription
125275	60-10-2, 10	inscription
125276	57-12-18, 33	inscription
125277	60-10-2, 6	inscription
125278	60-10-2, 13	inscription
125279	57-12-18, 25	inscription
125280	59-4-2, 10	inscription
125281	76-2-25, 5	inscription
125282	59-4-2, 13	inscription
125283	57-12-18, 11	inscription
125284	57-12-18, 80	
125285	86-6-21, 2	inscription
125286	60-10-2, 4	inscription
125287	76-2-25, 6	inscription
125288	57-12-18, 19	inscription
125289	60-10-2, 11	inscription
125290	59-4-2, 21	inscription
125291	60-10-2, 2	inscription
125292	59-4-2, 12	inscription
125293	60-10-2, 1	inscription
125294	59-4-2, 20	inscription
125295	76-2-25, 7	inscription
125296	57-12-18, 22	inscription
125297	57-12-18, 15	inscription
125298	60-10-2, 5	inscription
125299	86-6-21, 3	inscription
125300	60-10-2, 17	inscribed
125301	59-4-2, 11	inscription
125302	59-4-2, 28	inscription
125303	60-10-2, 18	inscription
125304	57-12-18, 24	inscription
125305	57-12-18, 13	inscription
125306	59-4-2, 15	inscription

125307	57-12-18, 9	inscription
125308	59-4-2, 7	inscription
125309	59-4-2, 6	inscription
125310	59-4-2, 30	inscription
125311	60-10-2, 16	
125312	59-4-2, 3	inscription
125313	59-4-2, 5	inscription
125314	57-12-18, 21	inscription
125323	86-6-21, 7	inscription
125324	57-12-18, 37	inscription
125330	59-4-2, 22	inscription
125718	57-12-18, 4	inscription
125719	57-12-18, 7	inscription
135693	60-10-2, 14	inscription

Neo-Punic stelae (61)

125021	57-12-18,62	
125043	59-4-2, 42	
125044	1880-1-30,12 (S.O.C.56)	inscription
125045	57-12-18,38	inscription
125050	57-12-18,43	inscription
125056	S.O.C. 4	inscription
125057	57-12-18,45	inscription
125062	57-12-18,63	
125063	57-12-18, 57	
125066	59- 4- 2,45 + 57-12-18,56	
125069	57-12-18,42	inscription
125070	59-4-2, 48	
125072	57-12-18, 54	
125073	57-12-18,64	
125075 + 125186	57-12-18,59	Lat. inscr.
125076	57-12-18,58	
125077	50-3-4, 39	
125078	59-4-2, 47	
125079	57-12-18, 61	
125090	58-6-3, 1	inscription
125095	59-4-2, 40	inscription
125098	57-12-18, 55	
125099	57-12-18, 41	inscription
125100	58-6-3, 2	inscription
125101	57-12-18, 52	
125102	59-4-2, 44	
125103	58-6-3-, 3	inscription
125104	57-12-18, 66	
125105	57-12-18, 47	inscription
125106	59-4-2, 46	
125115	50-3-4, 42	
125116	50-3-4, 43	
125117	57-12-18, 44	inscription
125118	59-4-2, 36	inscription
125119	59-4-2, 39	inscription
125174	59-4-2, 41	
125175	57-12-18, 40	inscription
125176	50-3-4, 41	
125177	57-12-18, 65	
125178	50-3-4, 36	
125179	50-3-4, 44	
125180	50-3-4, 37	
125181	50-3-4, 40	

125183	57-12-18, 53 + 59-4-2,38	inscription
125184	60-10-2, 121	
125185	60-10-2, 124	inscription
125186 +125075	60-10-2, 119	
125189	60-10-2, 118	Lat. inscr.
125190	59-4-2, 43	
125191	57-12-18, 39	inscription
125192	60-10-2, 120	
125193	60-10-2, 117	Lat. inscr.
125194	57-12-18, 48	inscription
125195	57-12-18, 49	inscription
125196	57-12-18, 46	inscription
125197	57-12-18, 60	
125198	59-4-2, 37	inscription
125200	57-12-18, 67	
125345	50-3-4, 38	
125981	57-12-18, 50	inscription
136681	58-6-3, 4	inscription

Appendix 1

The 'Honegger' Collection

In an attempt to uncover information on the provenance of the stelae, research in the archives of the British Museum revealed correspondence relating to the so-called 'Honegger Collection'.

This correspondence consists of a letter and memorandum of September/October 1848 from J.B. Honegger, addressed to Edward Hawkins (Keeper of Antiquities, 1826-60), and a similar memorandum to the Chariman of the Trustees, W.R. Hamilton. In the letter, Honegger submits twenty-seven Punic inscriptions to the Trustees for purchase. The memorandum gives details of provenance and rather flowery descriptions of some of the objects, which Honegger says are all inscribed.

Apparently the Museum was prepared to buy these objects, and there is a note to that effect in the Departmental correspondence, but for some reason the purchase was never finalised – perhaps because Honegger died before the sale was completed. (He died in 1849.)

Honegger states specifically in the memorandum that these monuments come from Maktar (or possibly Maghrawa). The monuments he describes are not in the British Museum. They include '... two bilingual inscriptions in Punic and Latin, one of which contains the name and lineage of a certain 'Lord of the Hamactharim' (*sic*) ... with a panegyric of his great virtues (being in one language). He also mentions three small columns with inscriptions and sculptures in relief.

After Honegger's death there was some dispute as to the ownership of the collection and, though it was again offered for sale, the Trustees declined to purchase.

It is likely that at some point Honegger turned his attention to other sites and it is probably from these that many of the neo-Punic stelae in the collection come. Nathan Davis acquired stelae from him which we know were not from Maktar[1] and so did Sir Thomas Reade. If any of the Museum stelae had been from Maktar it would have been known, for Honegger was very clear as to the provenance of the stelae he was submitting to the Trustees.

Letter and memorandum from J.B. Honegger to Edward Hawkins

2, Orange St. Red Lion Sqr. Holborn,
October 2, 1848.

Dear Sir

Agreeably to your kind request I take the liberty of presenting to you the faithful transcription of the Twenty-Seven Punic inscriptions, with eight drawings of the same monuments, a Memorandum and my proposition for their sale. I beg you to have the goodness to present them to the Trustees of the British Museum, for their learned consideration, on the first occasion of their reunion, and to inform the Trustees that I submit them to their generous and high patronage for purchase.

I trust the memorandum will furnish you with a just idea of the important and useful materials, which abound in this Collection of antiquities, for the advancement of Archeology and the illustration of a branch of Philology almost entirely obscured.

I am Dear Sir

Yours faithfully
J. B. Honegger

Memorandum

These Twenty-Seven epigraphical monuments – sacred relics of the literature of antiquity – were brought to light by my excavations upon the ruins of ages and are fragments of the learning and Theology of the ancient 'Hamactharim' (Macburebii Ptol.); they are, likewise, with regard to myself, a portion of the fruit of my labours and of an application of three Lustra to archeological researches on the classic land of Carthage.

These ruins, at a distance of eighty-one geographical miles W.S.W. from Carthage, are, by their own testimony, the vestiges of a City formerly great and important. Its name and that of its inhabitants, until now concealed from the Scientific world, appears for the first time upon these inscriptions, as also in the present memorandum, and written in two kinds of writing, exactly in this way:

'Hamactharim',

being the descendants of the Canaanites driven out by Joshua from the Promised Land, and who, fleeing to Egypt and afterwards expulsed therefrom, turned towards the West, and made the conquest of Libya, as far as the columns of Hercules, whence spring the Mighty Carthage.

On these monuments appear in graphic beauty, and with mostly precise inter-punctuation, the two kinds of Libo-Phoenician writing, both of which were the dominant Epigraphia until the times of the Roman conquest. These inscriptions are partly sepulchral and partly invocative, written in the idiom of Juba, 'the learned', the idiom concerning which Pliny clearly treats; and this is the Punic language, which during the last two Centuries, the most learned have exhausted their minds in attempting its development.

Now the basis, in order to arrive at this important end, are two Bilingual inscriptions in Punic and Latin (which are unique), one of which contains the name and lineage of a certain Lord of the 'Hamactharim', ... with a panegyric of his great virtues (being in one language), and which offers to philological science the first true knowledge of the powers of Letters, with their additional signs of both species of Libo-Phoenician writing, as well as lays the foundations of the just method of reading.

Amongst this collection are some monuments, which, besides the epigraphs, preserve Theological Dogmas, accompanied with Symbolical signs, the greater part of which are unknown to Philosophy.

In these representations appear the emblem of Deity, the image of the human soul, stars, and emblems of the elements of nature, and of protecting Gods, who, according to Diodorus Siculus, preside over the Constellations. These representations indicate the Knowledge and adoration of One Supreme God, the veneration for the Stars, and the intelligences that preside over the Stars – the Religion of the 'Hamactharim'.

But the monuments which contain more materials of this primitive religion are three small Columns, with invocative inscriptions and sculptures in relief, executed with art. They are the first Punic monuments of Religion ever discovered, which, besides their archeological interest, abound in new and important matters of Philology and Philosophy.

Upon these Columns appear, for the first time, the two triangles, the equilateral and the isosceles, placed so as at first sight to know their indication; that is to say, the equilateral is placed above the sun and the moon, and, according to the doctrine of Orpheus, the equilateral triangle is the triangle of Triune-Perfection, and compared by Henocrates to God; the isosceles triangle – once with two birds standing on the sides of the hypotheneuse, and once with the globe of the world within the hypotheneuse – is seen placed below the sun and the moon, and is the emblem of the air, the Element to which, according to Sanchoniathon, the Phoenicians sacrificed from time immemorial.

In addition to the above, by the placing of their Symbols and the composition of the number Three and the Triangular form, these monuments indicate as a mystic and sacred thing the number Three, a Dogma of ancient oriental philosophy, concerning which Plato formally reasons.

And one sees likewise, and which is particularly interesting, figured upon these monuments, the transmigration of the human soul. This is represented in the form of the Shadow of man, with hands extended above, and an aerial Body, the image of the soul, to which, as we learn from the inscriptions, libations were made.

These monuments, excavated from the ruins of ages, spread a new light from the Archives of the ancient East upon the high horizon of Science, resplendent with the greatness and glory of a people, who by their industry subdued nature, that they might light up the torch of science in the farthest West.

Notes

1 See Appendix 2.

Appendix 2

Extract of Letter from Nathan Davis to Lord Clarendon

Carthage, 29 June 1857

'My Lord,

... I have also great pleasure in informing your Lordship that I have succeeded in procuring a number of Punic antiquities discovered by Mr. Honnegger (*sic*) who resided in this country and died in London about 1849. A portion of these came from Zama the site of which is however debated among geographers although it is so famous for the defeat of Hannibal an event from which the real decline of Carthage commences to date. Another portion comes from Kef the ancient Succat-Beroth (Tabernacle of Venus) or Sicca Veneria chiefly remarkable for the infamous and immoral character of its inhabitants and for the part this city took in the Jugurthine war. The remainder come from Baja the ancient Vacca remarkable for its treacherous conduct towards the Romans and for the signal chastisement Metellus inflicted upon it for the same. Mr. Honegger having left no documents (except perhaps some guide to be found among his papers in possession of Mr. Vaux of the British Museum) it is impossible for me to classify these antiquities which I am now preparing for embarcation ...'

Appendix 3

Copy of Letter from Sir Grenville Temple

Transactions of the Royal Asiatic Society Vol 3 1835

Copy of a Letter from Sir GRENVILLE TEMPLE, BART., TO Lieut. General BENJAMIN FORBES, M.R.A.S., relative to a Phoenician Tombstone found at Maghrawah in Tunis, and presented to the ROYAL ASIATIC SOCIETY by Sir GRENVILLE TEMPLE. 7th of December 1833

Malta, 2d July 1833.

THE sepulchral stone with the Phoenician inscription, I found at *Magráwah*, a little village in the Beylik of Tunis, situated on the northern declivity of the range of hills, which separates *Muhadhar-al-Hammádah Waládd Ayár*, the ancient *Tucca* Terebenthina, from the plain of *Zirrz* inhabited by the *Bení Riss*, a branch of *Dthrídis*, and on which are seen the ruins of *Assura*, now called *Zanfúr*. I feel inclined to imagine that *Maghráwah* occupies the situation of one of those Libyo-Phoenician towns or villages which were never colonized by the Romans; for though we find several fragments of coarsely-executed bas-reliefs representing men and animals, evidently of a date anterior to the epoch when sculpture attained any degree of perfection, yet I saw not a single vestige of the workmanship either of the later Carthaginians or of their conquerors. Not the smallest fragment of either capital, frieze, or cornice is descernible. About an hour and a-half's distance from *Maghráwah*, in the direction of *Zanfúr*, is the small village of *Lheys*, where are found similar remains, mixed however with fragments of Roman inscriptions and sculpture.

The inscription, which I imagine to be written in one of the various Phoenician dialects, is valuable from its scarcity; for during a tour which I made through the whole of the interior of the Beylik, I only found seven or eight inscriptions which were not in Latin; and this one was all that I was enabled to bring away, the others being too large to be carried by a horse. It is I think a matter of astonishment that even these few have survived to the present day, when we recollect that the Romans did all in their power to obliterate, by the destruction of the institutions and monuments of the Punic power, all traces of the existence of that nation. The principle of '*delenda est Carthago*' was not confined to the destruction of the capital, but extended itself through all the provinces as far as the vast *Sahára*, effacing in all directions every thing which could in itself be thought to carry down to future ages the proof of the existence of Rome's greatest rival.

(Signed) GRENVILLE T. TEMPLE

Author's note

It is possible that the stela was acquired by Temple at Maghrawa, not Maktar. It is, however, clear from the internal evidence that the stela comes from Maktar. It may have been found and moved to Maghrawa when building stones were needed for the grand buildings of the local governor.

Appendix 4

Report on the Examination of Punic and Neo-Punic Stelae from Carthage

Andrew Middleton, Department of Scientific Research, The British Museum

Introduction

Approximately 200 stelae of the Museum's collection of Punic and neo-Punic stelae from North Africa were examined in order to identify the types of stone used. Each of the pieces was examined visually with the aid of a hand lens and a very small powder sample removed for testing with dilute acid (as an indicator for the presence of calcite, which effervesces briskly in the acid). The powder from a single stela (NPu21, 125044) was analysed by X-ray powder diffraction in order to provide an identification of the crystalline phases present in the stone. In addition a small fragment was removed from Pu74 (125303) for preparation as a thin section. This was examined using a petrographic microscope, in order to comment on the nature of the stone.

Results and discussion

Almost all of the sculptures were found to give a positive test for carbonate, indicating (in conjunction with the visual observations) that they are made of limestone. Visual observation also showed that several different types of limestone were used which differ in their texture, colour and hardness. Most are fine grained, ranging in colour from almost pure white through buff and yellow varieties to various shades of grey. Some of the stones are relatively soft and friable but many are compact and hard. The stone of individual pieces is generally quite uniform in character, although a few sculptures show cross-cutting veins, probably of calcite. The variations observed allowed only the most tentative of groupings to be established, and these seemed to show little concordance with possible cultural- or provenance- based associations. For example, there is a group of eight tomb-markers recognised by figures in a characteristic pose, carved into niches recessed into the stone slabs. These might have been expected to have been carved from the same type of stone. However it was observed that three of the sculptures are in rather similar pale buff-coloured limestones (TM4, TM5 and TM6); two are in very fine-grained stones which exhibit conchoidal fractures (TM3 and especially TM7); two are made from hard fine-grained grey-coloured stone (TM2, TM8) and the eighth (TM1) is in an unusual greenish- buff limestone containing dark brown (? marcasite) inclusions. Thus it would appear that several different sources of limestone (possibly all relatively local) were used to produce this group of sculptures which is comparatively well defined on the basis of the style of carving.

The few sculptures which appear to have been carved from stones other than the limestones discussed already are detailed below.

NPu21 (125044). The surface of this sculpture is very dark although the underlying stone is buff coloured. Both the acid test and XRD analysis indicated that it is somewhat calcareous but the XRD pattern indicated also the presence of gypsum. The gypsum may be an original constituent of the stone or it may have been deposited (especially at the surface?) during burial or weathering. The dark surface colour may again be due to an effect of weathering or perhaps to some past treatment such as waxing.

Pu72 (125217). The acid test on this stone indicated that it is a carbonate rock but visual observation suggests it is a marble (i.e. a metamorphosed limestone) rather than limestone.

Pu74 (125303). This stela is carved in a distinctive fine-grained red-brown stone. Macroscopic observation suggests that the red-brown coloration has been enhanced by some treatment such as the application of wax to the surface of the stone. Examination of the stone in thin section showed that it is a fossiliferous limestone.[1] In order to be consistent with the terminology applied to the other stelae, this stone is referred to here as a *fine-grained limestone.*

Conclusions

The study has shown that most of the sculptured stelae were carved from a range of fine-grained limestones. The observations did not lead to the recognition of well-defined petrographic groupings which could be correlated with associations of pieces based upon considerations of culture or provenance. Indeed, there was evidence that several different types of stone were used to produce a particularly well-defined group of tomb markers, perhaps implying the simultaneous exploitation of several different stone sources.

This apparent exploitation of several sources of stone does not necessarily imply, however, that any or all of the various types were imported; it is possible that all were relatively local. Further detailed investigation, including the examination of thin sections and the investigation of potential sources would have been necessary to resolve this question. However, the preparation of thin sections would have entailed the removal of small fragments from the sculptures and this was not felt to be justified within the context of the present investigation.

Recommendations on nomenclature

It is recommended that with the exceptions below, all of the stelae should be termed *fine-grained limestone* (or simply *limestone*). The nature of NPu21 (125044) is slightly doubtful and it should be termed *probably limestone*; Pu72 (125217) should be termed *marble*.

Note

1 A biomicrite in the terminology of R.L. Folk, Spectral subdivision of limestone types, *Memoirs of the American Association of Petroleum Geologists 1* (1962), 61-84

TM1

TM2

TM3

TM4

TM5

TM6

TM7

TM8

Pu1

Pu2

Pu3

Pu4

Pu5

Pu6

Pu6a

Pu7

Pu8

Pu9

Pu10

Pu11

Pu12

Pu13

Pu14

Pu15

Pu16

Pu17

Pu18

Pu19

Pu20

Pu21

Pu22

Pu23

Pu24

Pu25

Pu26

Pu27

Pu28

Pu29

Pu30

Pu31

Pu32

Pu33

Pu34

Pu35

Pu36

Pu37

Pu38

Pu39

Pu40

Pu41

Pu42

Pu43

Pu44

Pu45

Pu46

Pu47

Pu48

Pu49

Pu50

Pu51

Pu52

Pu53

Pu54

Pu55

Pu56

Pu57

Pu58

Pu59

Pu60

Pu61

Pu62

Pu63

Pu64

Pu65

Pu66

Pu67

Pu68

Pu69

Pu70

Pu71

Pu72

Pu73

Pu74

Pu75

Pu76

Pu77

Pu78

Pu79

Pu80

Pu81

Pu82

Pu83

Pu84

Pu85

Pu86

Pu87

Pu88

Pu89

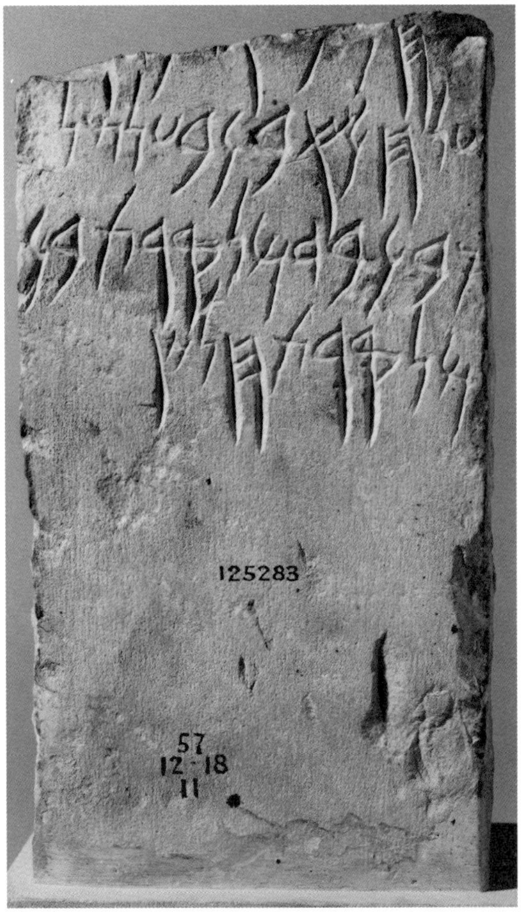

Pu90

Pu91

Pu92

Pu93

Pu94

Pu95

Pu96

Pu97

Pu98

Pu99

Pu100

Pu101

Pu102

Pu103

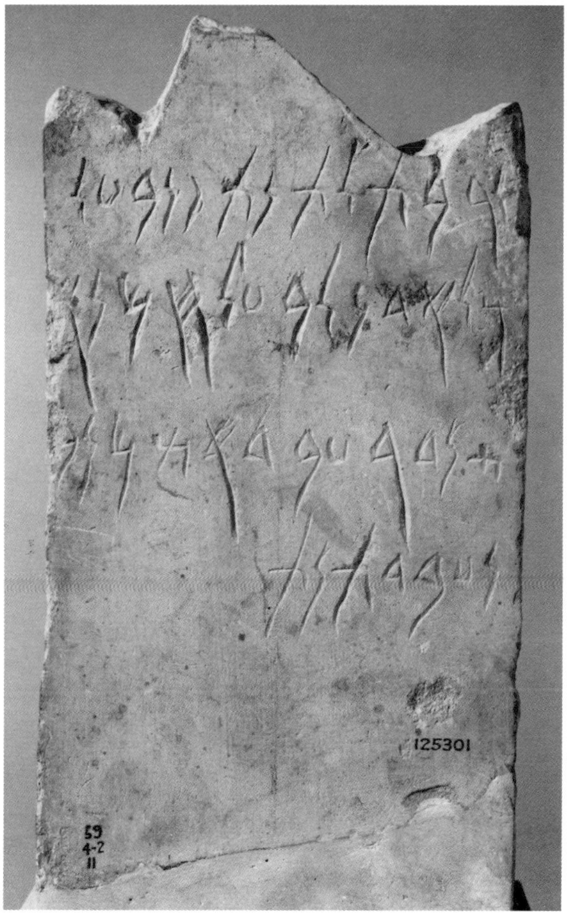

Pu104

Pu105

Pu106

Pu107

Pu108

Pu109

Pu110

Pu111

Pu112

Pu113

Pu114

Pu115

Pu116

Pu117

NPu1

NPu2

NPu3

NPu4

NPu5

NPu6

NPu7

NPu8

NPu9

NPu10

NPu11

NPu12

NPu13

NPu14

NPu15

NPu16

NPu17

NPu18

NPu19

NPu20

NPu21

NPu22

NPu23

NPu24

NPu25

NPu26

NPu27

NPu28

NPu29

NPu30

NPu31 and NPu43 joined together

NPu32

NPu33

NPu34

NPu35

NPu36

NPu37

NPu38

NPu39

NPu40

NPu41

NPu42

Note NPu 43 is illustrated joined to NPu31 with which it belongs

NPu44

NPu45

NPu46

NPu47

NPu48

NPu49

NPu50

NPu51

NPu52

NPu53

NPu54

NPu55

NPu56

NPu57

NPu58

NPu59

NPu60

NPu61